CYBERSECURITY
LIFE SKILLS FOR TEENS

Life Skills for the Digital Age

MARK LYND

Cybersecurity Life Skills for Teens

Life Skills for the Digital Age

Mark Lynd

Copyright© 2023

Published by Relevant Track, LLC.

ISBN: 979-8-218-19118-4

This book may be purchased for educational or business use. For more information, bulk orders, or a quote, please contact

mark@marklynd.com or visit www.marklynd.com

Cover by Angie at https://www.fiverr.com/pro_ebookcovers

CYBERSECURITY
LIFE SKILLS FOR TEENS

Table of Contents

Preface 1

Introduction 2

    The purpose and goals of this book 2

    How this book is organized..3

    Helpful smart tips 4

    Tips for getting the most out of this book 4

    Embark on the journey to becoming cybersecurity-savvy...............5

Chapter 1 7

    Welcome to the Digital World

        Getting the Hang of Cybersecurity Basics

Chapter 2 15

    Surfing the Web Safely

        Tips and Tricks for Smart Browsing

Chapter 3 21

    Email Security

        Keeping Your Email Accounts Secure and Avoiding Spam

Chapter 4 27

    Social Media Savvy

        Protecting Your Privacy and Reputation Online

Chapter 5 37

    Gaming Good Times

        Secure and Fun Online Gaming Experiences

Chapter 6 45

    The Social Scene

        Staying Safe on Social Media Platforms

Chapter 7 51

    Avoiding Sexting, and Sextortion

Chapter 8 57

    Shopping Smart

        How to Stay Safe While Shopping Online

Chapter 9 63

    Digital Hygiene

        Keeping Your Devices Clean and Secure

Chapter 10 71

Combating Cyberbullying and Building a Positive Online Reputation

Chapter 11 77

Safeguarding Your Digital Privacy and Security

Chapter 12 83

Wi-Fi Wisdom

Connecting Securely to Public and Private Networks

Chapter 13 87

Mobile Mastery

Securing Your Smartphone and Mobile Apps

Chapter 14 93

File Sharing

Understanding the Risks of File Sharing and How to Do It Safely

Chapter 15 99

Securing Alexa and Siri

Secure your IoT devices and protect your home network

Chapter 16 105

Identity Theft

Protecting yourself and what to do if it happens to you

Chapter 17 113

Future-Proofing Your Cyber Life

Keeping Up with Cybersecurity Trends and Threats

Chapter 18 119

Balancing Act

Understanding and Managing Your Digital Footprint

Chapter 19 127

Trust but Verify

Evaluating Online Sources and Spotting Misinformation

Chapter 20 133

Take off with a Career in Cybersecurity

In Closing...141

Acknowledgments...145

About Author 147

Preface

As an advisor to numerous kindergarten through 12th Grade schools (K-12), school districts, and universities on cybersecurity, I have had the privilege of working with many teen and young adult students, superintendents, chancellors, educators, and staff. Throughout my journey, I have been inspired by their dedication and hard work in navigating the ever-changing cybersecurity landscape. This inspiration led me to write "Cybersecurity for Teens."

I have also been inspired by my wife, Laura, and three daughters, Hailey, Brooke, and Taylor, who supported and assisted me during this book-writing expedition. Their ideas, suggestions, and occasional edits are greatly appreciated.

Cybersecurity is a journey, not a destination. It takes dedication and work to stay safe and secure in this challenging online world. This book is a guide to help teens develop the knowledge and skills they need to navigate this journey confidently.

My hope is that this book will empower teens to take control of their online safety and security. By developing a strong foundation in cybersecurity life skills, they will be well-equipped to face the cybersecurity challenges of the digital age.

So, let's embark on this journey together and discover the many rewards that come with being cyber-savvy.

Introduction

Welcome to the intriguing world of cybersecurity. The topic of cybersecurity continues to gain considerable attention worldwide as we are more connected than ever and continually growing our number of connections. With it, the number of threats we face grows.

Especially as a teenager, you are growing up in a time when the Internet, smartphones, and digital technology are integral parts of your daily life. You might use social media, online games, and more for entertainment, connecting with friends, and even learning. Technology is so ingrained that it is likely difficult to imagine a time when it wasn't part of your daily life.

While the benefits of the digital age are considerable, it is essential to recognize its drawbacks and hazards too. With cyber threats constantly changing and evolving, your privacy, personal information, and physical safety could all be negatively affected. That's why developing your cybersecurity skills is crucial to ensure your safe enjoyment of our digital world.

The purpose and goals of this book

- Equipping teens with essential cybersecurity knowledge and skills

This book is designed for teens like you, aiming to teach you the necessary knowledge and skills to navigate the digital world safely and confidently. We'll cover topics like creating strong passwords, safeguarding your personal information, recognizing phishing scams, and others.

- Empowering teens to navigate the digital landscape safely and confidently

By learning this book's crucial cybersecurity concepts and practices, you will be better equipped to make intelligent decisions in the digital world. Not only will this help you avoid potential pitfalls, but it will also empower you to take advantage of the many opportunities the digital world offers.

- Encouraging teens to become responsible digital citizens

As a teenager, you play a vital role in shaping the future of the digital world. This book aims to enable you to become a responsible digital citizen by promoting online safety, respecting the privacy of others, and being aware of the consequences of your actions in the digital space.

How this book is organized

- Description of the chapter structure

This book is divided into twenty chapters, each focusing on various aspects of cybersecurity. Some subjects, like cyberbullying, are covered in several chapters as it is in context within each of those chapters. The chapters are designed to be both informative and engaging, with real-life examples, illustrations, and practical tips to help you grasp the concepts more easily.

- Explanation of how the book progresses through various cybersecurity topics
- The book begins with foundational topics, like understanding online risks and creating strong passwords, then moves on to more advanced subjects, such as securing your home network and recognizing emerging cyber threats. This progression will help you build a solid understanding of cybersecurity as you work through the book.

Helpful smart tips

- Throughout the book, smart tips are meant to enlighten, emphasize or call out important ideas, suggestions, or concepts to accelerate the reader's cybersecurity life skills.

   This Smart Tip icon indicates these tips.

Tips for getting the most out of this book

- Encouragement to apply the skills learned in each chapter to real-life situations
- To truly master cybersecurity, applying the knowledge and skills you gain from this book to your everyday online activities is essential. Practicing what you learn will reinforce your understanding and develop good cybersecurity habits that will serve you well throughout your life.

- The importance of ongoing learning and staying informed about cybersecurity developments
- Cybersecurity constantly evolves, and staying informed about new threats and technologies is crucial. As you work through this book, remember that learning about cybersecurity is a journey, not a destination.
- Suggestions for engaging with others and sharing knowledge about cybersecurity
- One of the best ways to learn is by sharing knowledge and engaging with others. Talk to your friends, family, and teachers about cybersecurity, and discuss the topics you find most interesting or important. By engaging in cybersecurity conversations, you'll deepen your understanding and help others become more aware of the issues as well.

Embark on the journey to becoming cybersecurity-savvy

- Acknowledging the challenges and rewards of learning about cybersecurity
- Learning about cybersecurity may seem challenging at times, but it's well worth the effort. As you delve into the world of online safety and digital protection, you'll discover that being cybersecurity-savvy is both rewarding and empowering.
- The lifelong benefits of being knowledgeable about cybersecurity

- By investing your time and energy in learning about cybersecurity now, you're setting yourself up for lifelong success. The skills and knowledge you gain will keep you safer online and make you a more informed and responsible digital citizen. As technology evolves, your cybersecurity skills will be vital in your personal and professional life.
- A call to action for teens to embrace their role in creating a safer digital world
- Now, it's time for you to embark on this exciting journey to become a cybersecurity-savvy teen. By learning about cybersecurity and implementing your newfound knowledge, you'll protect yourself and contribute to a safer digital world for everyone.

So, buckle up, and let's dive into the fascinating world of cybersecurity! By the end of this book, you'll have the tools and knowledge to navigate the digital landscape safely, confidently, and responsibly. Are you ready? Let's get started!

Chapter 1

Welcome to the Digital World

Getting the Hang of Cybersecurity Basics

Hey there! This chapter is all about helping you understand the basics of cybersecurity. We'll review the most common threats you might face, how to identify weak spots in your online safety, and why taking personal responsibility is vital in protecting your digital life.

In today's hyper-connected world, cybersecurity is a must-have skill. It's about keeping our gadgets, networks, and personal info safe from digital attacks, sneaky access, and other harmful stuff. By getting a solid handle on cybersecurity, you'll be ready to explore the digital landscape with confidence and safety.

As you start this journey, you'll encounter many online risks. These can be anything from cybercriminals trying to swipe your private information to viruses and malware that can mess up your devices.

To help you stay protected, let's first go over some of the most common cybersecurity threats:

- Phishing attacks: These sneaky tricks usually come as emails or messages that try to fool you into giving up your personal info or clicking on dangerous links. They might pretend to be from legit organizations or people you trust, so always keep your eyes peeled for suspicious messages.
- Ransomware: This malicious software gets into your devices and locks up your files or entire systems, only giving them back if you pay a ransom. Ransomware attacks can be super bad, leading to significant data loss and money problems.
- Identity theft: When someone pretends to be you online, they can get into your personal info, bank accounts, and other sensitive stuff. Staying safe from identity theft means being extra careful and using strong security measures.

Knowing about these threats is just the first step. To really keep yourself safe, it's super important to know that you've got to take responsibility for your cybersecurity. This means doing things like:

- Always keep your software and devices up to date
- Using strong, unique passwords for each online account
- Being extra careful when clicking on links or downloading
- Not sharing too much personal info online

With a good grasp of cybersecurity basics, you'll be all set to take on the challenges of the digital world. In the following sections, we'll dive deeper into specific aspects of cybersecurity and give you some real-life smart tips for staying safe online.

Section 1: Multi-Factor Authentication

Extra Security for the Win!

Multi-Factor Authentication (MFA) adds another layer of security to your online accounts by making you prove your identity with two or more factors before letting you in and giving you access. This could be something you know (like a password), something you have (a security token or your phone), or something you are (like a fingerprint or face recognition).

Turning on MFA for your accounts will make it harder for anyone to break in, even if they have your password. Many online services now offer MFA, so use it whenever possible.

Smart Tip

Most major online platforms give you the option to utilize MFA to secure your account better.

Section 2: Backing Up Your Data

The Smart Move

It has never been easier to make backups of your important data. Backing up your data means making extra copies of all your essential items like photos, documents, and game saves, just in case something goes wrong. Computers and phones (yes, even smartphones) can break, get stolen, or be attacked by nasty viruses. By regularly backing up your data to a USB stick flash drive, external hard drive, or a secure cloud storage service (like Microsoft OneDrive, Apple iCloud, Box, Dropbox, etc.), you can make sure you don't lose anything important, even if the worst happens.

Smart Tip

You can even create a folder on your desktop for these backup services, so when you want to store a file, image, or video in the cloud to save space or to make sure you have a backup copy of your media, then drag the image onto the folder or copy and paste into the folder.

Section 3: Shopping Online

Don't Get Scammed!

Online shopping is super convenient, but it also comes with some risks. To make sure you don't get scammed or have your info stolen, follow these tips when shopping online:

- Stick to well-known websites and always check for a padlock (a little key lock) icon ☐ in the address bar, which means the site is more secure.
- Don't use public Wi-Fi for shopping, as it's easier for bad guys to snoop on you.
- Use a credit card or a secure payment service like PayPal, Venmo, or CachApp for extra protection. Most

credit cards provide payment protection in case of an issue.

- Another way to watch for malicious activity is to watch your bank statements for anything weird or unexpected.

Section 4: Stay in the Loop

Know Your Cyber Threats

The world of cybersecurity is constantly changing, with new threats continually popping up. You must keep learning about the latest trends and dangers to stay safe. Check out cybersecurity blogs, forums, newsletters, and news sites to stay informed.

Section 5: Social Media Safety

Protect Yourself and Your Friends

Social media is a great way to stay connected, but it can expose you to various risks. To keep yourself and your friends safe on social media, follow these guidelines:

- Tweak your privacy settings so only people you trust can see your posts and personal info.
- Be careful about accepting friend requests from strangers or friends you have already accepted a request from, as their account may be compromised.
- Don't overshare – the more you post about your personal life, the more info someone can use to target you.

- Refrain from posting revealing or questionable photos. They are out there forever and could be used to restrict you in some way in the future.
- If you see anything sketchy or mean, report it to the platform administrators.

Section 6: Viruses and Malware

Don't Let Your Devices Get Infected!

Viruses are still prevalent out there. Malware is short for "malicious software," and it's designed to sneak into your devices and cause all sorts of problems. To protect yourself from malware and viruses, follow these steps:

- Use a good antivirus/antimalware program and keep it updated.
- Don't click on weird links or download stuff from shady sources.
- Don't open spam emails, as they may be malicious.
- Make sure your operating system (OS) and software are always up to date.
- Be careful with USB drives and other removable media – they can be a sneaky way for malware to spread to other devices and networks.

Section 7: Password Power

Keep Your Accounts Locked Down

Your passwords are like the keys to your digital life, so you must ensure they're strong and secure. To create safe passwords, remember these tips:

- Mix it up with uppercase and lowercase letters, numbers, and special characters.
- Don't use easy-to-guess info like names, birthdays, or common phrases.
- Use a different password for each account (so if one gets hacked, the others are still safe).
- A password manager can help you create and store strong passwords without remembering them. Many password managers like 1Password and Dashlane will also create strong passwords for you to use for your online accounts.

Section 8: Encryption

What's the Big Deal?

Encryption is a fantastic way to protect your data by turning it into a secret code that can't be read without the correct key. It is often included or part of the service you subscribe to or use. Other services may allow you to utilize encryption as well. This ensures your info stays private and secure, whether on your devices or being sent over the internet.

You are learning about different secure communication tools and encryption methods to get the most out of encryption.

Then you will know how to keep your digital chats private and your sensitive info safe.

Chapter 2

Surfing the Web Safely

Tips and Tricks for Smart Browsing

What's up? This chapter will cover some excellent tips and tricks to help you browse the internet safely and smartly. The web is full of cool stuff but has many risks and dangers. By learning how to surf the web wisely, you'll be able to avoid online threats and enjoy exploring the digital world.

Section 1: Browsers and Privacy

Making the Right Choice

Your web browser is like a window into the internet; choosing the right one can make a huge difference in your online privacy and security. Some popular browsers like Google Chrome, Mozilla Firefox, Microsoft Edge, and Apple Safari offer privacy-focused settings and extensions to help you keep your browsing activities safe from prying eyes. Explore your browser's privacy options and tweak them to fit your needs.

Smart Tip

While most people default to using popular search engines like Google or Bing, these platforms often track your search queries and browsing history, potentially compromising your privacy.

You might consider using a more privacy-focused search engine like DuckDuckGo or Startpage. These search engines prioritize user privacy and do not track or store your personal information. This way, you can reduce the risk of your search queries and browsing history being used for targeted advertising or other purposes that may infringe on your privacy.

Section 2: URLs and Domains

Double-Check Before You Click

When browsing the web, paying attention to the URLs and domains of the websites you visit is essential. This helps you avoid sketchy sites and stay safe from phishing attacks. Remember these pointers:

- Check for HTTPS (A lock in the URL window that is locked) in the address bar, which means the website is secure. It doesn't mean it is a legit site, just that it is secure.

- Watch out for weird or suspicious-looking domains that could be trying to trick you. Bad actors often create copycat sites to trick people into submitting their credentials or other personal information.
- If you're unsure about a link, use a website safety checker to see if it's legit, or move on to another site.

Section 3: Public Wi-Fi

Convenience Comes at a Cost

Public Wi-Fi is a common way to access the Internet but it can also expose you to security risks. When you connect to an open network, like at a Starbucks or a public library, your online activities can be easily snooped on by bad guys. If you must use public Wi-Fi, follow these tips:

- Use a virtual private network (VPN) to encrypt your connection and keep your info safe.
- Stick to secure websites (look for the padlock icon in the address bar).
- Only log into sensitive accounts or do online shopping on public Wi-Fi if you absolutely have to, and if you do, be careful and aware.

Section 4: Online Ads

Don't Get Tricked by Clickbait

Online ads can be annoying, but they can also be dangerous. Some ads are designed to trick you into clicking on them and can lead to malware infections or scams. To stay safe from sketchy ads, keep these tips in mind:

- Use an ad blocker extension in your browser to block most ads from showing up. It is usually an add-in to your browser.
- Be extra careful with ads that seem too good to be true, like offers for free or amazing deals.
- If an ad looks suspicious, don't click on it, you are better safe than sorry.

Section 5: Downloads and Attachments

Proceed with Caution

Downloading files and opening email attachments can be risky if you're not careful. Malware and viruses can easily sneak into your devices through downloads and attachments. To avoid these threats, follow these guidelines:

- Stick to trusted sources like Apple, Google, Spotify, and Microsoft for downloading software, music, and other files.
- Be wary of email attachments, especially if they're from someone you don't know or aren't expecting.
- Scan all downloads and attachments with your antivirus software before opening them.
- A good practice is if you are unsure or wary of a potential download, then don't download it.

Section 6: Online Gaming

Keep It Fun and Secure

Online gaming is a blast, but it can also open you up to some online risks. To keep your gaming experience fun and secure, remember these safety tips:

- Use a strong and unique password for each gaming account.
- Utilize MFA if available for extra security.
- Be careful with in-game chat – don't share personal info or click on suspicious links.
- Keep your gaming devices and software up to date with the latest security patches.

Section 7: Cyberbullying

Stand Up and Speak Out

Cyberbullying is a serious issue that affects many teens online, and we will cover it deeper in Chapter 5. It's important to recognize and address cyberbullying to keep the internet a fun and safe place for everyone. If you or someone you know is being targeted, follow these steps:

- Don't respond to the bully – it usually makes things worse.
- Save evidence like screenshots or messages to show to an adult or report the behavior.
- Talk to a trusted adult, like a parent or teacher, about the situation.

- Report the bullying to the website, app, or platform where it's happening.

Section 8: Being a Good Digital Citizen

Your Role in Online Safety

As a teen, you have a unique role in the online world. You're responsible for your safety, being a good digital citizen, and setting a positive example for others. Here's how you can contribute to a safer and more inclusive online community:

- Be kind and respectful to others online, just like in real life.
- Think before you post – taking back once something is online can be challenging. Too often, an emotional post is followed by regret and concern.
- Stand up against cyberbullying and support those who are being targeted.
- Share your online safety knowledge with your friends and family when the opportunity arises.

Now that you've learned some great tips and tricks for safe browsing and added to your knowledge and habits, you can enjoy all the amazing things the internet offers while staying protected from its risks. Happy surfing!

Chapter 3

Email Security

Keeping Your Email Accounts Secure and Avoiding Spam

In today's digital world, email has become an essential communication tool. From connecting with friends to receiving notifications from social media and school assignments, our inboxes are constantly buzzing. With the increasing importance of email, it's crucial to keep our accounts secure and learn to spot potential threats. This chapter will guide you through the basics of email security, help you recognize and avoid scams, and teach you how to protect your account with strong passwords and multi-factor authentication.

Section 1: Understanding the Basics of Email Security

Email security is about more than just choosing a strong password. It involves understanding how cybercriminals can access your account, steal your personal information, or spread malware. Emails can be a treasure trove of sensitive data, so staying vigilant and protecting your account from potential threats is essential.

Cybercriminals often use deceptive tactics to trick you into revealing your personal information or clicking on harmful links. Email scams and phishing attacks are two common methods they employ. Here are some tips to help you recognize and avoid these threats:

- Watch for suspicious sender addresses: Scammers often use email addresses that resemble those of legitimate companies or individuals. Look for slight misspellings, odd characters, or inconsistencies in the sender's address.

- Beware of urgent or threatening language: Phishing emails often create a sense of urgency or fear to prompt you to act quickly without thinking. Be cautious of emails that demand immediate action or threaten consequences.

- Don't click on unknown links or download unexpected attachments: Scammers often use links and attachments to spread malware or direct you to fake websites designed to steal your information. Hover over the link with your cursor to see the actual URL before clicking on it. If you need clarification on an attachment, verify its legitimacy with the sender before opening it.

- Look for spelling and grammar mistakes: Phishing emails often contain errors in spelling or grammar that can be a giveaway of their illegitimate nature.

Legitimate companies and organizations typically proofread their messages before sending them out.

- Verify the email's authenticity: If you need clarification on the legitimacy of an email, contact the sender or company directly using their official contact information. Don't use links, phone numbers, or email addresses provided in the suspicious email.

Smart Tip

If you are unsure or suspect an email, you can always check the email address by right-clicking on the email address (not the link), which will show you the address. If the domain shown after the @ doesn't match a legitimate domain or seems suspect, stay safe and delete or report the email. Be careful: Many bad actors make slight changes to a domain name to seem similar and legit, but it is not.

Section 2: Managing Your Inbox

Using Filters and Organizing Your Emails Effectively

Keeping your inbox organized can help you spot potential threats and reduce the risk of falling for scams. Here are some tips for managing your inbox effectively:

- Use filters and folders: Most email services offer filtering options that allow you to sort incoming emails based on specific criteria. You can create folders for different categories, such as personal, school, or promotional emails, and set up filters to automatically sort incoming messages.

- Unsubscribe from unwanted emails: If you're receiving too many promotional emails or newsletters, consider unsubscribing to reduce clutter in your inbox. This can also decrease the chances of accidentally clicking on a malicious link in a spam email.

- Report spam and phishing emails: If you receive a suspicious email, report it to your email provider. It helps them improve their spam filters and protect other users from similar threats.

Section 3: Protecting Your Email Account

Using Strong Passwords and Enabling Multi-Factor Authentication

A strong password and multi-factor authentication can significantly increase the security of your email account. Here's how to implement these measures:

- Create a strong password: Use a combination of uppercase and lowercase letters, numbers, and special characters to create a unique and complex password. Avoid using easily guessable information, like your name, birthdate, or common words. Update your password regularly and avoid using the same password across multiple accounts.

- Enable multi-factor authentication: Multi-factor authentication (MFA) adds an extra layer of security by requiring additional verification methods, such as a code sent to your phone or a fingerprint scan, before granting access to your account. This makes it much more difficult for an unauthorized person to gain access, even if they have your password.

- Be cautious when using public Wi-Fi: Public Wi-Fi networks can be insecure, making it easier for cybercriminals to intercept your data. Avoid accessing your email or other sensitive accounts when connected to public Wi-Fi, or use a virtual private network (VPN) to encrypt your internet connection.
- Keep your devices and software updated: Regularly update your devices and software, including your email client and web browser, to protect against known security vulnerabilities.
- Be mindful of the information you share: Be cautious about sharing personal or sensitive information via email. Once you send an email, you lose control over who sees its contents. If you must share sensitive information, consider using an encrypted messaging app or another secure method.

Understanding the basics of email security, recognizing and avoiding scams, managing your inbox effectively, and protecting your account with strong passwords and multi-factor authentication, can reduce the risk of falling prey to cybercriminals.

Staying informed about potential threats and maintaining a proactive approach to online safety will help you enjoy a more secure email experience.

Chapter 4

Social Media Savvy

Protecting Your Privacy and Reputation Online

Social media is a huge part of our lives, right? It's fun to connect with friends and family, share our thoughts and experiences, and meet new people. But, like anything else online, it's important to be smart and safe when using social media. This chapter will explore tips and tricks for staying safe on social media while enjoying everything it offers.

Section 1: Privacy Settings

Your First Line of Defense

Privacy settings are super important when it comes to social media. They help you control who can see your posts, pictures, and personal info. Here are some pointers for managing your privacy settings:

- Familiarize yourself with the privacy settings on each platform you use. The default settings are often not to your benefit.
- Set your profiles to private or friends-only, so only people you trust can see your stuff.
- Regularly review and update your settings to ensure they meet your needs.
- If there is a privacy or terms update that you have to acknowledge to use the platform, then it is wise to check and verify that your settings are still set to your liking. Google, Microsoft, Facebook, Instagram, Twitter, TikTok, and others do this often.

Section 2: Friending and Following

Quality over Quantity

When it comes to your online social circle, it's important to be selective about whom you friend or follow. This can help protect your privacy and keep your online experience positive. Keep these tips in mind:

- Only accept friend requests from people you know and trust in real life.
- Be cautious about following accounts that seem suspicious or too good to be true.
- Don't feel obligated to follow or friend everyone who requests it. It's okay to be picky!

- Be wary of an additional invite request from someone you know and previously followed, as their account might have been hacked.

Section 3: Sharing Content

Think Before You Post

Sharing content on social media is fun, but it's essential to be mindful of what you're putting out there. Here are some guidelines to help you make intelligent choices about what to share:

- Avoid posting personal information like your address, phone number, or school.
- Be cautious about sharing your location, especially if your profile is public.
- Remember that once you post something, it can be hard to take back – think twice before sharing anything that could be embarrassing or hurtful.
- Any photos you post may resurface later, so be careful when considering what photos to post. That post of a keg handstand, or a revealing swimsuit can show up during a job interview down the line.

Section 4: Passwords and Account Security

Lock It Down

Keeping your social media accounts secure is crucial for protecting your privacy and personal info. Here's how to lock down your accounts and keep hackers at bay:

- Use strong, unique passwords for each of your social media accounts. Change them occasionally to have more robust protection.

- Enable multi-factor authentication (MFA) for added security.

- Be cautious about using third-party apps that request access to your accounts – make sure they're legit and trustworthy.

- Be cautious about clicking on links or downloading attachments from unknown sources, as they may contain malware or lead to phishing websites.

Smart Tip

Use a passphrase instead of a traditional password. Passphrases are typically longer than regular passwords, making them more difficult for attackers to crack through brute force methods.

Consider a memorable sentence or phrase with multiple words, numbers, and special characters to create a strong passphrase. For example, instead of using a simple password like "P@ssw0rd1," consider using a passphrase like "MyDogAte2Tacos!" This passphrase is more secure due to its length and complexity, and it's also easier for you to remember because it tells a story.

Section 5: Online Interactions

Keep It Positive and Respectful

The way you interact with others on social media can have a significant impact on your online experience. By being positive and respectful, you can help create a safe and supportive digital community. Here are some ideas:

- Treat others online how you'd like to be treated in real life with kindness and respect.
- If someone is being rude or negative, it's okay to unfriend, unfollow, or block them.
- Stand up against cyberbullying and support those who are being targeted.
- Be careful about disclosing potentially negative or controversial information to others.

Section 6: Dealing with Online Harassment

Know Your Options

If you experience online harassment or cyberbullying, knowing what to do and where to turn for help is important. Keep these steps in mind:

- Don't engage with the harasser – it might make things worse.
- Save evidence, like screenshots or messages, to show to an adult or report the behavior.
- Talk to a trusted adult, like a parent or teacher, about the situation.

- Report the harassment to the social media platform where it's happening.

By following these tips and staying aware of the potential risks, you can enjoy social media's fun while staying safe and secure. So, go ahead and snap that selfie, share that meme, or post that update; remember to keep your smarts about you and make intelligent choices.

Section 7: FOMO and Social Media Addiction

Finding Balance

It's no secret that social media can be addictive, and FOMO (Fear of Missing Out) is real for many teens. But it's important to find balance and not let social media take over your life. Here are some tips for maintaining a healthy relationship with social media:

- Set reasonable boundaries for when and how long you use social media each day.
- Make time for offline activities, like hanging out with friends and family, playing sports, or pursuing hobbies.
- Remind yourself that people often only share their "highlight reels" online, and it's okay if your life isn't picture-perfect all the time.
- Create a "mindful scrolling" ritual. This approach encourages you to be more intentional and aware of the time spent on social media platforms.

Here's how to create a mindful scrolling ritual:

o Set a timer: Before you start browsing your social media feeds, set a timer for a specific amount of time, such as 10 or 15 minutes.

This will help you become more aware of the time spent on social media and prevent mindless scrolling.

o Purposeful engagement: As you scroll through your feed, make it a point to only engage with content that truly resonates with you or brings value to your life. This could be liking a post, leaving a thoughtful comment, or sharing the content with someone else. By being more selective, you'll be less likely to get lost in the endless stream of content.

o Reflection: When the timer goes off, take a moment to reflect on your scrolling session. What did you learn? How did the content you engaged with make you feel? By being more mindful and reflective, you'll be better equipped to manage your social media use and develop healthier habits.

Section 8: Geotagging and Location Sharing

Be Mindful of Your Digital Footprint

While sharing your location or checking in at your favorite hangout spots can be fun, you must be mindful of the risks of revealing your whereabouts online.

- Turn off geotagging features in your social media apps so your photos and posts don't automatically include your location.
- Be cautious about sharing your location in real-time or "checking in" at specific places, as this can make it easier for someone to track your movements.

- Limit the use of location-sharing apps, such as Find My Friends, Life360, or Snapchat's Snap Map, to close friends and family members.

Smart Tip

Use generic location tags: While it's tempting to tag your exact location when posting photos, using a generic tag is safer. For example, tag the city or neighborhood instead of tagging the specific restaurant, park, or venue you're visiting. This prevents others from pinpointing your exact whereabouts while still allowing you to share your experiences with friends.

Section 9: Staying Informed

Keeping Up with Social Media Safety Trends

Just like the online world is constantly changing, so are the best practices for staying safe on social media. Make a habit of staying informed about the latest safety tips, privacy features, and potential risks. Here's how:

- Follow reliable sources and organizations that share information about online safety.
- Talk to your parents, teachers, or other trusted adults about what you learn and any concerns.
- Share your knowledge with your friends and help create a safer, more informed online community.

By staying in the loop and continuously learning about social media safety, you can maximize your online experience while minimizing the risks. Loaded with this knowledge, you'll be well on your way to becoming a social media pro who knows how to stay safe and enjoy all the benefits these platforms offer.

Chapter 5

Gaming Good Times

Secure and Fun Online Gaming Experiences

What's up, gamers? We all know that playing video games is a blast, especially when we can join our friends or even make new ones in online multiplayer matches. However, as with anything online, staying safe and protecting ourselves while gaming is crucial.

Let's learn some tips and tricks to help you enjoy online gaming while securing your personal info and accounts.

Section 1: Choosing the Right Games

Fun and Safe Options

Before diving into the world of online gaming, it's essential to choose games that are not only fun but also safe to play. Here are some tips for picking suitable games:

- Look for games with a strong reputation for being secure and respecting players' privacy.

- Read reviews and get recommendations from friends to find games that match your interests.
- Always download games from official sources, like the game's website or reputable app stores, to avoid malware and scams.
- Adjust your privacy settings on streaming services to limit the visibility of your viewing history, playlists, and recommendations.

Section 2: In-Game Communication

Chat with Care

Chatting with other players can be a fun part of online gaming, but you must be cautious about what you share and whom you chat with. Keep these guidelines in mind:

- Use a gaming-specific username that doesn't reveal your real name or personal info.
- Avoid sharing personal details, like age, location, or school, in public chats or with strangers.
- Be respectful and kind to others, and report any toxic or harassing behavior.
- Be careful, as quite a few gamers are not who or what you think they are.

Section 3: Passwords and Account Security

Keep Your Gaming Accounts Safe

Your gaming accounts can be a goldmine for hackers, so keeping them locked down and secure is important. Follow these tips to protect your gaming accounts:

- Use strong, unique passwords for each gaming platform and game you play.
- Enable multi-factor authentication (MFA) whenever it's available.
- Avoid linking your gaming accounts to social media or other third-party services.

Section 4: Gaming on the Go

Mobile Device Security

Mobile gaming is very popular, but keeping your devices and personal info safe while playing on the go is essential. Here's how:

- Keep your device's operating system and apps updated with the latest security patches.
- Only download games and apps from reputable sources, like official app stores.
- Be cautious when connecting to public Wi-Fi networks – use a VPN to encrypt your data and protect your privacy.

Section 5: In-Game Purchases and Microtransactions

Spend Wisely

Many games offer in-game purchases and microtransactions for virtual items or currency. While spending a little money on your favorite games is okay, being smart about your spending is important. Consider these tips:

- Set a budget for your gaming expenses and stick to it.
- Use prepaid game cards or virtual credit cards to limit your financial exposure.
- Be cautious about sharing your payment information with gaming platforms or websites. It is important to make sure they're secure and reputable.

Section 6: Dealing with Online Harassment and Toxic Behavior

Know Your Options

Unfortunately, online gaming can sometimes involve toxic behavior or harassment. If you experience this, knowing how to handle it and where to turn for help is essential. Keep these steps in mind:

- Mute or block the player(s) involved to avoid further interaction.
- Report the behavior to the game's developers or moderators, providing any evidence you have.
- Talk to a trusted adult, like a parent or teacher, about the situation and seek their guidance.

By following these guidelines and staying aware of potential risks, you can enjoy all the excitement of online gaming while keeping your personal information and accounts safe. So, gear up, level up, and prepare to dominate the gaming world.

Section 7: Streaming and Content Creation

Share Your Gaming Adventures Securely

If you're interested in sharing your gaming experiences through streaming or content creation, it's essential to do so safely. Here are some tips for secure gaming content creation:

- Use a separate email address and username for your streaming or content creation accounts that don't reveal your personal information.
- Be cautious about what you show on camera – avoid capturing your surroundings or personal items that could reveal your identity or location.
- Monitor your chat and comments using moderation tools and a trusted team of moderators to keep things positive and safe.

Section 8: Securing Your Home Network

Keep Your Entertainment Hub Safe

Your home network plays a crucial role in your gaming and streaming experiences. Keep your network secure with these pointers:

- Change the default login credentials for your router and use a strong and unique password.

- Enable WPA2 encryption on your Wi-Fi network, if available, to protect your connection from unauthorized access. This is usually a checkbox on the configuration page for your Wi-Fi router or access point. If unsure, contact your broadband service provider for more details.
- Set up a visitor guest network, keeping your main network secure and separate.
- Keep your router's firmware updated, as updates often include security enhancements. Firmware is the base software embedded in the hardware by the manufacturer that provides the base capabilities.

Smart Tip

Consider using a virtual private network (VPN) to secure your connection, especially if you game or stream on public Wi-Fi networks.

Section 9: Connecting with Fellow Gamers

Building a Safe Gaming Community

As you dive deeper into the world of gaming, you'll likely want to connect with other players who share your interests. Here's how to build a safe and fun gaming community:

- Join reputable gaming forums, Discord servers, or social media groups focusing on your favorite games.

- Get to know fellow gamers before sharing personal information, and remember that not everyone online is whom they claim to be.
- Create or participate in positive, inclusive gaming spaces that promote kindness and respect.

Section 10: Staying Informed

Keep Up with Gaming Security Trends

Just like in other areas of cybersecurity, staying informed about the latest gaming security trends and best practices is essential. Make a habit of:

- Following gaming news sources and cybersecurity experts to stay updated on potential risks and safety tips.
- Sharing what you learn with friends and fellow gamers helps create a more secure gaming community.
- Continuously evaluate your gaming habits and practices to ensure you stay safe and secure.

By being proactive and staying informed, you'll be better equipped to enjoy your gaming adventures while minimizing risks. You're well on your way to becoming a cybersecurity-savvy gamer who knows how to have a blast while staying safe online.

Chapter 6

The Social Scene

Staying Safe on Social Media Platforms

Hey there, social butterflies! Social media is a huge part of our lives, from catching up with friends to sharing our latest adventures. It's important to remember that we must be cautious about how we use social media to keep ourselves and our information safe. In this chapter, we'll walk you through tips and tricks to help you stay secure while navigating your favorite social media platforms.

Section 1: Setting Up Your Profiles

Building a Safe Social Media Presence

Creating a social media profile is your first step into the world of online socializing. Keep these tips in mind when setting up your accounts:

- Use a unique username and email address that don't reveal your real name or personal information.
- Ensure your profile picture doesn't contain identifiable information, like your school or address.
- Be cautious about what you include in your bio. Keep it fun, but avoid sharing too many personal details.

Smart Tip

Nearly all social platforms collect your personal information, which is often used in ways you might not be aware of; therefore, it is essential to stay informed. Example: If you use a social platform like TikTok that has reported ties to the Chinese government, your data, and information is being collected and may be used later, potentially putting you or your information at risk.

Section 2: Privacy Settings

Keeping Your Info and Posts Under Wraps

Adjusting your privacy settings is crucial to staying safe on social media. Here's how to lock down your accounts:

- Review the privacy settings for each platform you use and set them to restrict who can view your profile and posts.
- Disable location tagging on your posts to avoid revealing your whereabouts.

- Consider limiting who can send direct messages or friend requests to people you know.

Section 3: Posting Wisely

Share Your Life, but Protect Your Privacy

Social media is about sharing photos, updates, and thoughts, but it's important to think before posting. Keep these guidelines in mind:

- Avoid sharing personal information, like your phone number, address, or school name.
- Be mindful of your photos' backgrounds, ensuring they don't reveal any identifiable details.
- Remember that anything you post online can be seen by anyone, even with privacy settings in place, so be cautious about what you share.
- Once it is online, it stays online regardless of if you delete it. The image has already made a digital footprint, or someone may have taken a screenshot before you deleted it.
- Avoid talking or posting about upcoming travel using dates and times, as it may alert bad actors to opportunity.

Section 4: Friend Requests and Followers

Choose Your Online Circle Carefully

Growing your social media network can be fun, but being selective about whom you connect with is essential. Here are some suggestions:

- Only accept friend requests or follow requests from people you know and trust.
- Regularly review your friends and followers list, removing anyone who seems suspicious or whom you no longer want to be connected with.
- Be cautious about accepting friend requests from strangers, even if they appear to have mutual friends.
- Be cautious of accepting friend requests from friends who you thought were already in your circle. Likely their profile has been hacked or duplicated by someone stealing information.

Section 5: Dealing with Cyberbullying and Online Drama

Stand Up and Stay Safe

Unfortunately, social media can sometimes be a breeding ground for cyberbullying and drama. If you find yourself in a challenging situation, here's what to do:

- Save any evidence of the bullying or harassment, like screenshots or messages.
- Block or unfriend the person(s) involved to prevent further interaction.
- Report the situation to the social media platform, and talk to a trusted adult, like a parent or teacher, for guidance and support.

By following these tips and staying vigilant about your online safety, you can enjoy social media's social fun while keeping yourself and your   information   secure.

Chapter 7

Avoiding Sexting, and Sextortion

Section 1: Introduction to sexting and sextortion

As texting and online chatting have become integral to many of our teenagers' lives, it brings new challenges and risks. These risks include an increased prevalence of sexting, and sextortion among teens, which is very concerning. It is important to ensure more education and awareness of these issues to help combat them.

- The potentially devastating risks and consequences of these activities need more attention.
- Sexting and sextortion can have serious consequences, including emotional, social, and legal repercussions. It is essential for teens to understand these risks and take steps to protect themselves and their peers.

Section 2: Understanding sexting

Sexting has been a growing concern for parents, teachers, and law enforcement. It is especially difficult to recognize unless someone comes forward.

- Sexting involves sending sexually explicit images, videos, or messages through electronic means such as smartphones or computers. It can take many forms, from suggestive texts to explicit photos or videos.
- There are various reasons teens may engage in sexting, including curiosity, peer pressure, and seeking attention or validation. Understanding these motivations can help in preventing and addressing sexting incidents.
- Sexting can have severe legal consequences, especially for minors. Sharing explicit content of someone under the age of consent can be considered child pornography, leading to criminal charges and potentially lifelong consequences.
- Aside from legal consequences, sexting can lead to emotional and social repercussions, such as feelings of guilt, shame, and embarrassment. It can also damage relationships and reputations, as shared content can quickly spread among peers or even become public.

Smart Tip

Document and save evidence: If you discover a compromising image or message has been shared without your consent, take screenshots of the content, including any conversations or messages related to the incident.

Section 3: Recognizing and avoiding sextortion

Sextortion uses threats or manipulation to obtain sexually explicit content, favors, or money. It can take many forms, from blackmailing someone with explicit content to coercing someone into engaging in sexual acts.

- Perpetrators of sextortion may use various tactics, such as threats to share explicit content, manipulation of emotions, or exploiting personal information to coerce victims into complying with their demands.

- Sextortion cases can vary widely, but they often involve a perpetrator gaining access to explicit content or personal information and using it to control and exploit the victim. Examples include cases where victims have been coerced into providing more explicit content or engaging in sexual acts.

- To protect yourself from sextortion, be cautious about sharing personal information and explicit content, even with people you trust. Keep your online accounts secure with strong passwords, and be mindful of potential red flags in online interactions.

Section 4: Responding to sexting and sextortion incidents

If you or someone you know becomes a victim of sexting or sextortion, it is essential to act quickly. Preserve any evidence, such as messages or images, and report the incident to a trusted adult, school counselor, or law enforcement.

- Depending on the nature of the incident, it may be necessary to involve law enforcement, school officials, or online platforms. Ensure you provide all relevant evidence and information to help address the situation effectively.

- Victims of sexting or sextortion may experience emotional distress and require support. Reach out to friends, family, counselors, or mental health professionals for help coping with the incident's emotional aftermath.

- Learning from these experiences can help prevent future incidents. Reflect on what led to the situation and consider how you can change your online behaviors to minimize risks. Share your experiences with others to raise awareness and help prevent similar incidents from happening.

Section 5: Encouraging safe and responsible behavior

Open communication about sexting and sextortion is crucial in creating a safe and supportive environment.

Discuss these issues with peers, parents, and educators to ensure everyone knows the potential risks and how to respond if they or someone they know is affected. Here are some other safeguards:

- Promote a culture of respect and consent in online interactions by being mindful of your own behavior and encouraging others to do the same. Practice empathy, consider the potential consequences of your actions, and respect the boundaries of others.
- Education and awareness play a significant role in preventing sexting and sextortion incidents by understanding the potential risks and consequences, as well as knowing how to recognize and respond to these situations, teens can be better equipped to navigate the digital landscape safely.
- Staying informed about sexting and sextortion risks is essential for protecting yourself and others. Continue learning about these issues and be proactive in adopting safe online behaviors.

Sharing your knowledge and experiences can significantly impact the safety and well-being of others. By raising awareness about sexting and sextortion, you can help create a safer digital environment for everyone.

Chapter 8

Shopping Smart

How to Stay Safe While Shopping Online

The internet is a treasure trove of amazing finds, from scoring the latest fashion trends to snagging the best deals on tech gadgets. But, as with everything else online, keeping your cybersecurity practices in hand while you shop is essential. We'll guide you through the ins and outs of safe online shopping so that you can spend wisely with less worry.

Section 1: Finding Reputable Online Retailers

Shop with Confidence

The first step to safe online shopping is to find trustworthy retailers. Here's how to ensure the shops you're browsing are legit:

- Look for familiar and reputable retailers, such as well-known department stores like Walmart or Target, online giants like Amazon, or official brand websites like Nike and Land's End.

- Check for customer reviews and ratings, giving you an idea of other shoppers' experiences with a retailer.
- Pay attention to the site's URL: a secure site should have "https://" and a padlock icon in the address bar.
- Be aware that many copycat sites have subtle changes to trick you into entering your personal information and credentials.

Section 2: Creating Secure Accounts

Protect Your Personal Information

Once you've found a reliable retailer, you'll likely need to create an account to make purchases. Keep these tips in mind when setting up your shopping accounts:

- Use a unique email address and strong password for each account. Refrain from using the same login credentials across multiple sites.
- Enable multi-factor authentication (MFA) if the retailer offers it. This adds an extra layer of security to your account.
- Be cautious about the information you provide when setting up your account. Only enter the necessary details and avoid oversharing personal information.

Section 3: Shopping Safely

Keep Your Transactions Secure

Now that you're all set with a secure account, it's time to start shopping! Follow these guidelines to keep your transactions safe:

- Ensure your computer, smartphone, or tablet runs the latest operating system and has updated security software.

- Only shop on secure, password-protected Wi-Fi networks or your mobile carrier's network (LTE, 4G, and 5G). Avoid making purchases while connected to public Wi-Fi.

Smart Tip

Double-check the retailer's return policy and shipping fees before purchasing, so you know what to expect if you need to return an item or how much you'll pay for shipping.

Section 4: Payment Security

Guard Your Financial Information

When paying for your online purchases, protecting your financial information is crucial. Keep these pointers in mind:

- Use a credit card or a secure payment service like PayPal, Venmo, or CashApp for online transactions. These options offer more protection and fraud prevention than debit cards or direct bank transfers.

- Check your bank statements regularly for any suspicious activity or unauthorized charges. If you spot anything unusual, report it to your bank immediately.
- Be cautious when entering your payment information and double-check that the site is secure, and never save your credit card details on a retailer's website.

Section 5: Recognizing Scams and Fraud

Don't Get Fooled by Online Trickery

Unfortunately, online shopping can also be a breeding ground for scams and fraud. Stay alert and protect yourself with these tips:

- Be wary of deals that seem too good to be true. It could be a scam if a price seems unrealistically low or the deal seems too good.
- Watch out for phishing emails that appear to be from retailers or delivery services, asking you to click on links or provide personal information. Instead, visit the retailer's website directly to check on your order status. Phishing emails include a link that, when clicked on, unleashes a virus or other malware without the user who clicked on it knowing.
- Report any suspicious activity, like fake retailer websites or phishing emails, to the appropriate authorities or online platforms.

Smart Tip

Pay attention to the site's URL in the address bar and ensure it matches the brand or company you are shopping from. Especially if you are buying tickets to concerts, sporting events, or other live events, this is a common area where bad actors try to scam teens.

Section 6: Safeguarding Your Online Purchases being shipped

You have made your purchase and are eagerly awaiting the package. Keep your deliveries safe with these helpful tips:

- If you won't be home during the delivery window, consider having your package sent to a trusted neighbor, a family member's house, or your workplace (if allowed).

- Set up package tracking notifications, so you'll know when your delivery is on its way and when it has been delivered.

- Look into package delivery services offered by carriers, like UPS My Choice or FedEx Delivery Manager, which may allow you to customize your delivery options or choose a pickup location.

Smart Tip

Review your bank/credit card statements weekly/monthly for strange/unusual authorizations. Verify the purchases are purchases you made and recognize. Scammers will steal $.99 or $1.99, so they go under the radar.

Chapter 9

Digital Hygiene

Keeping Your Devices Clean and Secure

Like your room or locker, your digital devices need regular care and maintenance to stay clean and secure. In this chapter, we'll cover essential digital hygiene practices to help you keep your devices running smoothly and protect your personal information from potential cyber threats.

Section 1: The Importance of Software Updates

Staying One Step Ahead

Updates may seem like a nuisance, but they're crucial for keeping your devices secure and functioning properly. Here's why they matter:

- Updates often include security patches that fix vulnerabilities hackers could exploit.

- New features and improvements can enhance your device's performance and user experience.
- Regularly updating your software demonstrates responsibility and good digital citizenship.

Section 2: How to Update Your Devices

A Step-by-Step Guide

Updating your devices is easier than you might think. Follow these steps to ensure you're running the latest software:

- For smartphones and tablets, check for updates in the "Settings" app, usually under "Software Update" or "System Update."
- On computers, use the built-in update utility for your operating system (e.g., Windows Update or macOS Software Update).
- Remember to update your apps and web browsers, too! These can usually be updated through the app store or within the app itself.

Section 3: Password Management

Your First Line of Defense

Creating and managing strong passwords is a crucial aspect of digital hygiene. Here's how to up your password game:

- Use unique, complex passwords for each account. Avoid easily guessed phrases like "password123" or your pet's name.

- Consider using a passphrase, a sequence of random words, or a sentence that is easy for you to remember but hard for others to guess.
- Use a password manager to help you securely track all your passwords.

Section 4: Multi-Factor Authentication

An Extra Layer of Security

Multi-factor authentication (MFA) or the older but still moderately effective two-factor authentication (2FA) adds an additional layer of security to your accounts, making it harder for hackers to gain access. Here's how to get started with MFA:

- Check if your accounts offer MFA in the security settings, and enable it whenever possible.
- Choose your preferred MFA method, such as receiving a text message or using an authentication app.
- Remember that MFA is not foolproof, so continue to practice good digital hygiene in other areas.

Section 5: Protecting Your Devices from Malware

Staying Safe in a Digital World

Malware is malicious software that can infect your devices and cause many problems. It can be delivered or activated via phishing or by a hacker placing it on your device or network.

Here's how to protect yourself from malware:

- Install and regularly update reputable antivirus software on your devices.

- Be cautious when downloading apps, files, or attachments from unknown sources.
- Avoid clicking on suspicious links, even if they appear to come from a friend or trusted source.

Section 6: Safe Web Browsing

Navigating the Internet Responsibly

The internet is full of valuable information and entertainment but has its dangers. Here's how to stay safe while browsing the web:

- Use a reputable web browser, such as Google Chrome, Mozilla Firefox, or Apple Safari, and keep it updated.
- Be cautious when visiting unfamiliar websites, especially if they have a poor reputation or lack security features.
- Learn to recognize and avoid phishing attempts, which are scams that try to trick you into revealing your personal information.

Smart Tip

If you receive an email from an unfamiliar sender claiming to be from a legitimate organization or acquaintance, take a few minutes to verify their identity by searching their name, email address, or social media profiles. Look for any discrepancies or suspicious activity that may indicate a spear-phishing attempt.

Section 7: Securing Your Home Network

A Digital Fortress

Your home network is your first line of defense against online threats, so it's essential to keep it secure. Here are some tips for securing your home network:

- Change the default login credentials for your router to a unique username and strong password.
- Enable Wi-Fi Protected Access (WPA3) encryption to secure your wireless network.
- Regularly update your router's firmware to patch any security vulnerabilities.
- Consider setting up a guest network for visitors to prevent unauthorized access to your main network.

Section 8: Safeguarding Your Personal Information

Privacy Matters

Protecting your personal information is a crucial aspect of digital hygiene. Here are some tips to help you keep your data private and secure:

- Be cautious about sharing sensitive information online, such as your address, phone number, or Social Security number.
- Please review the privacy settings on your social media accounts and adjust them to limit the information you share with others.

- Be aware of how your data is being used by your apps and services, and consider deleting accounts or apps that collect too much information.

Section 9: Physical Security

Don't Forget Your Devices

While digital hygiene is essential, protecting your devices physically is also crucial. Keep these tips in mind to safeguard your gadgets:

- Never leave your devices unattended in public places; always lock them when not in use.
- Use strong, unique passcodes or biometric security features like fingerprint or facial recognition to lock your devices.
- Consider investing in a protective case or screen protector to prevent accidental damage.

Section 10: Digital Detox

Finding Balance in a Connected World

Digital hygiene is not just about keeping your devices clean and secure; it's also about maintaining a healthy balance between your online and offline life. Here's how to practice digital detox:

- Set boundaries for your screen time, such as limiting yourself to a specific number of hours per day or having designated device-free times.
- Be mindful of how you use your devices and prioritize activities that promote genuine connections and personal growth.

- Remember that taking a break from technology is okay, whether for a few hours, a day, or even a week. Your digital life will still be there when you return.

By following these guidelines regarding digital hygiene, you can surf the web, connect with friends, and enjoy your digital life while knowing you're taking the proper steps to stay safe and secure.

Chapter 10

Combating Cyberbullying and Building a Positive Online Reputation

In this digital age, it's essential to be aware of the potential risks and dangers lurking online, including cyberbullying and the consequences of a negative online reputation. This chapter will guide you on recognizing and combating cyberbullying, building a positive online presence, and ensuring a safe and enjoyable online experience.

Section 1: Understanding Cyberbullying

Cyberbullying is a form of harassment that occurs online, often involving repetitive, hostile behavior targeting a specific individual. It can take various forms, including:

- Sending mean or threatening messages via email, text, or social media.

- Spreading rumors or sharing private information about someone.
- Posting embarrassing photos or videos without permission.
- Creating fake profiles or websites to ridicule or impersonate someone.

Section 2: Recognizing the Signs of Cyberbullying

Identifying the signs of cyberbullying is crucial to addressing the problem early. Watch out for these red flags:

- Receiving unkind messages, comments, or emails.
- Noticing rumors or gossip being spread about you online.
- Experiencing sudden changes in your online friendships or interactions.
- Feeling anxious, upset, or embarrassed by things happening online.

Section 3: Dealing with Cyberbullying

If you're experiencing cyberbullying, taking action and standing up for yourself is essential. Here's how:

- Don't retaliate: Responding to the bully angrily or aggressively may only fuel their behavior. Instead, remain calm and collected.
- Save the evidence: Keep a record of any harassing messages, posts, or images to help you report the incident.

- Report the bullying: Inform a trusted adult, such as a parent or teacher, and report the incident to the relevant social media platform or website.
- Block the bully: Prevent further contact by blocking the bully on social media, email, or text.
- Take care of yourself: Remember that it's not your fault, and practice self-care by talking to friends, engaging in hobbies, or seeking professional help if needed.

Smart Tip

Before reacting to a potentially hurtful comment or message, take a moment to consider the context and the person behind the screen. By practicing empathy, you can better navigate online interactions and avoid becoming involved in or perpetuating cyberbullying.

Section 4: Building a Positive Online Reputation

Your online reputation can significantly impact your personal and professional life. Here's how to build a positive online presence:

- Please think before you post: Be mindful of what you share online, as future employers, college admissions officers, or your future self may see it.
- Adjust your privacy settings: Control who can see your content by adjusting the privacy settings on your social media accounts.

- Create a positive digital footprint: Share content that showcases your interests, achievements, and talents. This can help you build a strong personal brand.
- Google yourself: Regularly search your name online to monitor your online presence and address any negative content that may appear.

Section 5: Being a Responsible Digital Citizen

A responsible digital citizen treats others with respect, both online and offline, and acts ethically and responsibly in the digital world. Follow these guidelines to be a good digital citizen:

- Be respectful: Treat others how you want to be treated, and avoid cyberbullying or online harassment.
- Protect your privacy: Be cautious about sharing personal information online and respect the privacy of others.
- Be a critical thinker: Evaluate the information you encounter online and be aware of potential scams, hoaxes, or fake news.
- Stand up for others: If you witness cyberbullying or other harmful online behavior, support the victim and report the incident.

By understanding cyberbullying, recognizing the signs, and knowing how to deal with it, you can protect yourself and others from the harm it causes.

Chapter 11

Safeguarding Your Digital Privacy and Security

As you spend more and more time online, it becomes crucial to understand how to protect your digital privacy and security. This chapter will teach you the essential steps you need to take to ensure your online activities remain private and secure from prying eyes, hackers, and potential identity theft.

Section 1: Importance of Digital Privacy and Security

Your digital privacy and security are vital for several reasons:

- Protecting your personal information from falling into the wrong hands.
- Preventing unauthorized access to your accounts and devices.
- Ensuring a safe and enjoyable online experience.
- Preserving your digital reputation and future opportunities.

- Browsing online or checking your email always maintains a healthy level of skepticism. Question the authenticity of messages, posts, or offers that seem too good to be true or come from unknown sources.

Section 2: Creating Strong and Unique Passwords

One of the most effective ways to protect your online accounts is using strong and unique passwords. Here's how to create them:

- Make it long: Aim for at least 12 characters in length.
- Mix it up: Use a combination of uppercase and lowercase letters, numbers, and special symbols.
- Avoid common words: Stay away from dictionary words, names, or easily guessed phrases.
- Use a passphrase: Consider creating a passphrase consisting of multiple random words.
- Be unique: Avoid using the same password for multiple accounts.

Section 3: Protecting Your Devices

Your devices can be vulnerable to unauthorized access, viruses, and malware. Take these steps to secure them:

- Keep software up to date: Regularly update your operating system, apps, and antivirus software.
- Use a reliable antivirus program: Choose a reputable antivirus solution to protect your devices from malware and other threats.

- Enable a firewall: A firewall can help block unauthorized access to your device.
- Lock your devices: Use a password, PIN, or biometric lock (like fingerprint or facial recognition) to secure your devices.
- Be cautious with public Wi-Fi: Avoid using public Wi-Fi for sensitive activities like online banking, and consider using a virtual private network (VPN) for added security.

Section 4: Maintaining Privacy on Social Media

Your social media presence can reveal a lot about you. Follow these tips to protect your privacy:

- Adjust privacy settings: Customize the privacy settings on your social media accounts to control who can see your posts and personal information.
- Think before you post: Be mindful of the content you share and how it may impact your digital reputation.
- Limit personal information: Avoid sharing sensitive information like your home address, phone number, or date of birth.
- Be selective with friend requests: Only accept requests from people you know and trust.
- Review your profiles regularly: Periodically review your social media profiles to ensure they accurately reflect your current interests and values.

Section 5: Identifying and Avoiding Scams and Phishing Attacks

Scams and phishing attacks are designed to trick you into revealing sensitive information or installing malware on your devices. Stay alert and follow these guidelines:

- Be cautious with unsolicited emails: Don't click on links or download attachments from unknown senders.

- Look for warning signs: Poor grammar, spelling errors, and suspicious email addresses can be red flags for phishing attempts.

- Verify the sender: If unsure about an email, contact the sender directly through a known, trusted method to confirm its legitimacy.

- Protect your information: Never share your passwords, social security number, or financial information via email or text.

Smart Tip

Be cautious when presented with opportunities, and conduct thorough research before taking action. Look for reviews, reach out to trusted friends or family for advice, and learn to recognize the red flags of potential scams (e.g., unrealistic promises, requests for personal information, or pressure to act quickly).

By implementing these strategies and remaining vigilant, you'll be well on your way to safeguarding your digital privacy and security. So, enjoy your online activities, knowing you're taking the necessary steps to protect yourself and your personal information in the digital   world.

Chapter 12

Wi-Fi Wisdom

Connecting Securely to Public and Private Networks

The internet has become an integral part of our lives, and Wi-Fi networks help us stay connected wherever we go. But knowing the risks and best practices when connecting to public and private networks is essential. In this chapter, we'll cover how to use public Wi-Fi safely, secure your home Wi-Fi network, and explore the benefits of using a Virtual Private Network (VPN).

Section 1: Understanding the Risks of Public Wi-Fi Networks

Public Wi-Fi networks can be found in many places like coffee shops, libraries, and airports. While they're convenient, they also come with risks:

- Unencrypted connections: Public Wi-Fi networks often lack encryption, making it easy for hackers to intercept and read your data.

- Rogue hotspots: Cybercriminals can set up fake Wi-Fi networks that resemble legitimate ones, tricking users into connecting and exposing their data.

- Snooping and sniffing: Hackers can use special software to monitor and capture data transmitted over public Wi-Fi networks.

- Malware distribution: Public networks can be used to spread malware to connected devices.

Section 2: Best Practices for Using Public Wi-Fi Safely

To protect yourself when using public Wi-Fi, follow these best practices:

- Turn off sharing: Disable file and printer sharing on your device to prevent unauthorized access to your files.

- Use HTTPS: When browsing the web, ensure the website uses HTTPS, which encrypts data between your device and the site.

- Enable two-factor authentication (2FA): Use 2FA on your accounts for an extra layer of security.

- Keep software up to date: Regularly update your operating system and apps to protect against vulnerabilities.

- Don't access sensitive information: Avoid checking your bank account or entering passwords while connected to public Wi-Fi.

Smart Tip

Many devices have settings that allow them to connect to available Wi-Fi networks automatically. While this can be convenient, it can also be risky in a public place like a coffee house. Disable the auto-connect feature on your device to prevent it from connecting to potentially unsecured or malicious networks without your knowledge.

Section 3: Securing Your Home Wi-Fi Network

Your home Wi-Fi network should be secure to protect your devices and personal information. Here's how to secure it:

- Change the default username and password: Replace the default login credentials for your router with strong, unique credentials.
- Update the router's firmware: Regularly check for and install firmware updates to patch security vulnerabilities.
- Enable WPA3 encryption: Use the latest Wi-Fi encryption standard, WPA3, to secure your network.
- Disable remote management: Turn off remote access to your router's settings to prevent unauthorized access.
- Set up a guest network: Create a separate network for guests to use, keeping your primary network secure.

Section 4: The Benefits of Using a Virtual Private Network

A Virtual Private Network (VPN) is a service that encrypts your internet connection and routes it through a remote server, providing several benefits:

- Enhanced privacy: A VPN hides your IP address and location, making your online activities more private.
- Increased security: VPNs encrypt your data, protecting it from hackers and other threats, even on public Wi-Fi networks.
- Bypassing geo-restrictions: VPNs allow you to access content that may be blocked or restricted based on your location.
- Avoiding bandwidth throttling: Some ISPs may slow your connection for specific activities, like streaming. A VPN can help prevent this by hiding your online activities from your ISP.

By using public Wi-Fi safely, securing your home Wi-Fi, and understanding the benefits of a VPN, you can connect securely to public and private networks. It will help protect your personal information and enjoy a safer online experience in public.

Chapter 13

Mobile Mastery

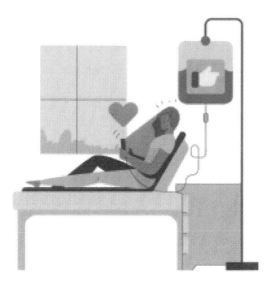

Securing Your Smartphone and Mobile Apps

Our smartphones have become an integral part of our daily lives, allowing us to communicate, stay informed, be entertained, and access an array of essential services, all within a compact, portable device.

While these technological marvels undoubtedly make our lives easier, they also introduce new risks and vulnerabilities that we must be aware of and address. This chapter will guide you through the process of securing your smartphone and mobile apps, ensuring that you can confidently navigate the digital world while keeping your data and privacy intact.

Section 1: Smartphone Security Basics

The first step in securing your smartphone is to ensure that you have a strong, unique passcode or biometric security feature, such as fingerprint or facial recognition, enabled on your device. This helps protect your phone from unauthorized access in the event it falls into the wrong hands. Additionally, be sure to enable your phone's auto-lock feature, which will automatically lock the device after a specified period of inactivity.

It's equally important to maintain the security of your smartphone by installing regular software updates provided by the manufacturer. These updates often contain essential security patches that protect your device from known vulnerabilities and threats. Remember to install and update reputable antivirus and anti-malware software on your smartphone.

Furthermore, exercise caution when downloading and installing mobile apps. Stick to official app stores, such as the Apple App Store or Google Play Store, and avoid downloading apps from third-party sources, which may harbor malicious software. Always check an app's rating, read user reviews, and research the developer to ensure you download a trustworthy application.

Section 2: Evaluating App Permissions and Privacy Settings

Mobile apps often request access to various features and data on your smartphone, such as your location, contacts, or camera. While some of these permissions are necessary for the app to function correctly, others may be invasive or pose a risk to your privacy.

It is essential to evaluate the permissions an app requests and determine whether they are genuinely needed for the app's purpose. If an app's permissions seem excessive or suspicious, consider looking for an alternative app that respects your privacy.

To manage app permissions, navigate to your smartphone's settings and locate the privacy or app permissions section. Here, you can review the permissions granted to each app and revoke access to specific features if necessary. Make it a habit to periodically review your app permissions to ensure your data remains secure.

Additionally, take the time to explore and configure an app's privacy settings to suit your preferences. This may include disabling ad tracking, limiting data sharing, or opting out of location tracking when it's not required. By taking control of your privacy settings, you can minimize the potential for your data to be misused or exposed.

Smart Tip

Before installing an app, read reviews and research to see if other users have experienced privacy issues. Be cautious of apps with a history of requesting unnecessary permissions or mishandling user data. Check the app's reputation and the developer's credibility to help you decide if granting the permissions it requests is safe.

Section 3: Preventing Unauthorized Access to Your Device

In addition to securing your smartphone with a strong passcode or biometric security feature, there are other measures you can take to prevent unauthorized access to your device. One such method is enabling multi-factor authentication (MFA) for your online accounts, such as email, social media, and banking apps.

MFA adds an extra layer of security by requiring you to enter a one-time code, typically sent via text message or generated by an authentication app, in addition to your password when logging in.

Be cautious when connecting to public Wi-Fi networks, as they may be unsecured and could expose your data to potential cybercriminals. Avoid conducting sensitive tasks like online banking or logging into personal accounts when connected to public Wi-Fi. If you must use public Wi-Fi, consider using a Virtual Private Network (VPN) to encrypt your internet connection and protect your data from prying eyes.

Moreover, be wary of phishing attempts targeting your smartphone, such as text messages or instant messages containing suspicious links or requests for sensitive information. Like phishing emails, be cautious with unsolicited messages, and never click on suspicious links or provide personal information to unknown sources.

Section 4: Steps to Take if Your Phone is Lost or Stolen

Despite our best efforts, accidents can happen, and smartphones can be lost or stolen. Acting quickly to protect your data and privacy is vital in such situations. Here are some steps you can take if your phone is lost or stolen:

- Locate your device: Most smartphones have built-in device tracking features, such as Find My iPhone for iOS or Find My Device for Android. These services allow you to locate your phone remotely, providing it's connected to the internet, and the feature is enabled.

- Lock your device: If you cannot locate your phone, use the device tracking feature to remotely lock it and display a custom message with your contact information in case someone finds it.

- Wipe your device: If you cannot recover your phone or believe it's been stolen, use the device tracking feature to erase all data on your smartphone remotely. This will help protect your personal information from being accessed by unauthorized individuals.

- Report the loss or theft: Contact your mobile carrier to report the loss or theft of your device. They can help disable your phone's service, preventing unauthorized use. Additionally, file a report with the local police department, as they may be able to assist in recovering your device.

- Change your account passwords: As a precautionary measure, change the passwords for any accounts that were accessible from your lost or stolen smartphone, especially those that contain sensitive information, such as email, banking, or social media accounts.

- By following the guidance in this chapter, you'll be well on your way to securing your smartphone and mobile apps, allowing you to enjoy the convenience and connectivity they offer with peace of mind.

Chapter 14

File Sharing

Understanding the Risks of File Sharing and How to Do It Safely

Section 1: Introduction to file sharing

A. Definition and common uses of file sharing

As our lives become increasingly digital, sharing files with friends, family, and classmates has become essential to everyday communication. File sharing involves transmitting digital files, such as documents, images, videos, and music, from one person to another over the Internet.

In today's interconnected world, file sharing plays a crucial role in collaborating on projects, socializing, and accessing various forms of digital content. Whether working on a school assignment, sharing vacation photos, or streaming your favorite movies, understanding how to share files safely and responsibly is more important than ever.

Section 2: The risks associated with file sharing

File sharing can expose you to various security threats, such as malware, viruses, and other harmful software. Cybercriminals often use seemingly innocuous files to spread their malicious software, which can lead to severe consequences, including data loss or identity theft.

- Sharing files without proper security measures can inadvertently expose sensitive or personal information. This exposure can result from sharing files containing hidden data, accidentally uploading private files to public platforms, or failing to set appropriate privacy settings on shared folders.

- Sharing copyrighted material, such as movies, music, or software, can lead to serious legal consequences if used or distributed without permission. Downloading or distributing copyrighted content without the owner's consent is illegal and can result in fines, lawsuits, or criminal charges.

- Sharing files on unsecured networks or platforms can make your data vulnerable to unauthorized access and data breaches.

Section 3: Types of file sharing platforms and their security features

- Cloud-based file-sharing services (e.g., Google Drive, Dropbox) store your files on remote servers, allowing you to access and share them from any device with an internet connection. These services often offer robust security features like encryption, access controls, and activity tracking. However, reviewing their privacy policies is essential to understand how your data is stored and protected.

- Peer-to-peer (P2P) file-sharing networks (e.g., BitTorrent)
Allow users to connect directly to each other and share files without relying on a centralized server. While P2P networks can be a convenient way to share large files, they are often associated with higher security risks due to the lack of centralized control and the prevalence of illegal content.

- Direct messaging and file-sharing apps (e.g., WhatsApp, Telegram) enable users to send files directly to each other through encrypted messages. These apps often use end-to-end encryption, ensuring only the intended recipient can access the shared files. However, it's essential to be cautious about the files you receive and the people you interact with to avoid potential security threats.

Before choosing a file-sharing platform, evaluating its security and privacy features is crucial. Look for platforms that offer encryption, access controls, and a transparent privacy policy. Additionally, research the platform's reputation and history of data breaches to ensure your files will be protected.

Section 4: Tips for safer file sharing

A. Limiting access and using password protection

- When sharing files, limit access to only the intended recipients. Use password protection or access controls to ensure only authorized individuals can view or download the shared files. This practice helps prevent unauthorized access and maintains the confidentiality of your information.

- Before sharing sensitive files, consider encrypting them to add an extra layer of protection. Encryption scrambles the data in a file, making it unreadable without the proper decryption key. This step ensures that even if an unauthorized party intercepts the file, they cannot access its contents.

- Keep your software, including your operating system and file-sharing applications, up to date to ensure you're protected against known security vulnerabilities.

- Be cautious when receiving files from unknown sources or suspicious emails. Verify the sender's identity and scan the files for malware before opening them. If you need clarification on a file's authenticity, contact the sender to confirm the content and its source.

Smart Tip

When sharing files with others, consider using a file-sharing service that allows you to set an expiration date for the sharing link. By doing this, you can limit the time your files are accessible, reducing the chances of unauthorized access.

Section 5: Educating others about safe file-sharing practices

- Share your knowledge about safe file-sharing practices with your friends and family members. Encourage them to adopt responsible habits, such as using secure platforms, encrypting sensitive files, and verifying the sources of shared files.

- Promote a culture of cybersecurity awareness and responsibility in your school and community by participating in educational events, starting or joining cybersecurity clubs, and sharing resources on safe file-sharing practices.

- Foster a sense of collective responsibility for online safety by discussing cybersecurity topics with your peers and sharing tips and experiences. Encourage open communication and collaboration to develop a community of informed and responsible digital citizens.

Section 6: File sharing requires diligence

- As file sharing continues to play a significant role in our digital lives, understanding the associated risks is crucial. Knowing potential security threats, privacy concerns, and legal implications can help you make informed decisions about your file-sharing activities.

- Adopting safe file-sharing practices protects your data and contributes to a more secure digital environment for everyone. Taking the necessary precautions can help prevent cyberattacks, data breaches, and the spread of malicious software.

- Continuously updating your knowledge about file sharing and cybersecurity is essential to staying safe online. Stay informed about new developments, trends, and best practices to ensure you're always prepared to responsibly protect your data and navigate the digital world.

This chapter covers the basics of file sharing, its risks, and tips for sharing files safely. By understanding the potential dangers and implementing safeguards, you can minimize the risks and enjoy the benefits of file sharing responsibly.

Chapter 15

Securing Alexa and Siri

Secure your IoT devices and protect your home network

Section 1: Introduction to the Internet of Things

As we venture deeper into the digital age, an increasing number of devices around us are becoming interconnected. This phenomenon is known as the Internet of Things (IoT). IoT devices are everyday objects equipped with sensors, software, and the ability to connect to the internet, allowing them to collect and share data. Examples include smart home devices like Siri, Alexa, smart appliances like your refrigerator or washing machine, wearable fitness trackers, and even internet-connected toys.

IoT devices have quickly become commonplace in our lives, streamlining tasks and providing us with valuable insights. From controlling the temperature in our homes to monitoring our heart rates, these devices have made our lives more convenient and efficient.

Section 2: Understanding the security risks associated with IoT devices

As the number of IoT devices continues to grow, so does the potential for security vulnerabilities. Since these devices are often designed to focus on functionality, security may be overlooked. This leaves IoT devices susceptible to cyberattacks, which can have serious consequences, such as unauthorized access to personal information and even physical harm.

- IoT devices can pose significant risks to our privacy, as they often collect and transmit sensitive data. Additionally, weak security measures can make IoT devices an entry point for cybercriminals, potentially compromising the security of your entire home network.

- Keeping your IoT devices updated with the latest firmware and security updates is critical. One crucial step in securing IoT devices is ensuring they are running the latest firmware and security updates. Manufacturers often release updates to fix vulnerabilities, so installing them promptly is essential.

- Many IoT devices come with default usernames and passwords, which hackers can easily exploit. To protect your devices, change the default login credentials to something unique and strong.

- Some IoT devices have features and services you may not need, which can present additional security risks. Review your device's settings and disable unnecessary features to reduce potential vulnerabilities.
- Monitoring and controlling access to your IoT devices
- Please keep track of who can access your IoT devices and ensure that only trusted individuals can interact with them. Use strong authentication methods and be cautious when granting access to others.

Smart Tip

Is Siri or Alexa listening to all of your conversations? To minimize the risk of accidental or unintended voice commands being picked up by your smart speaker, set up a "mute" schedule when the device is not in use, like when you're at school or asleep. Many smart speakers have a physical mute button, but you can also use smartphone apps or automation tools to schedule automatic mute times. This way, your Alexa or Siri device won't accidentally listen in or be triggered by conversations or background noise when you don't need it.

Section 3: Protecting your home network

To keep your home network secure, use strong, unique passwords for your Wi-Fi network, and enable encryption (such as WPA3) to protect data transmitted between devices.

Your router is the gateway to your home network, so keeping its firmware current is vital. Check for updates regularly and install them as needed.

Consider creating a separate Wi-Fi network for your IoT devices. This isolates them from your primary network, reducing the potential damage in case of a security breach.

Adopt network security best practices, such as disabling remote management, enabling a firewall, and monitoring network traffic for unusual activity.

Section 4: Educating others about IoT security

- Spread the word about IoT security by discussing the risks and best practices with friends, family, and peers. Encourage open discussions and share your experiences to help others stay safe.
- Promote a culture of responsibility when it comes to IoT devices. Encourage those around you to adopt safe practices and to stay informed about potential threats.
- Work towards creating a community that values cybersecurity. Engage in conversations, participate in local events, or even start a cybersecurity club at your school.

Section 5: Looking ahead: the future of IoT security

As IoT devices become more prevalent, new security technologies and practices will continue to emerge. Stay informed about these developments and be prepared to adapt as necessary.

- The digital landscape constantly evolves, so staying informed about new threats and security measures is essential. Regularly research and update your knowledge to ensure you're always prepared.
- Teens play a crucial role in shaping the future of the digital world. By staying informed and adopting responsible practices, you can create a safer environment for everyone.

Section 6: Be aware and be safe when using IoT devices at home

As IoT devices become more integrated into our lives, it's vital to understand and address the security risks they pose. You can protect your devices and personal information by educating yourself and adopting secure practices.

- Responsible security practices protect your IoT devices and home network and contribute to a safer digital world for everyone.
- Always remain vigilant and proactive when it comes to online safety and security.
- Share your knowledge, experiences, and insights to help others stay safe and to contribute to a more secure digital future.

Embrace this responsibility and work towards fostering a culture of security for you and your family when using home-focused devices that include technologies like Alexa and Siri.

Chapter 16

Identity Theft

Protecting yourself and what to do if it happens to you

Section 1: Introduction to identity theft

- It's crucial to understand the risks associated with our online lives. One of the most significant threats is identity theft, which occurs when someone steals your personal information and uses it for fraudulent purposes, like opening accounts or making purchases in your name.

- Identity theft has become increasingly common due to the vast amount of personal information available online. With the expansion of social media and digital transactions, it's more important than ever to be vigilant in protecting your sensitive information.

Section 2: How identity theft occurs

Identity thieves employ various tactics to access your information. These methods include phishing scams, data breaches, and even old-fashioned dumpster diving. They also use social engineering techniques to trick you into revealing sensitive data.

Section 3: The potential consequences of identity theft

- The financial consequences (e.g., credit score, debt) of identity theft can be severe. Victims may find themselves saddled with debt, facing a damaged credit score, and struggling to regain control of their finances. In some cases, it can take years to recover from the financial repercussions fully.

- Identity theft can also have a profound emotional and psychological impact on its victims. Many people feel violated, vulnerable, and stressed after their identity has been stolen, leading to anxiety, depression, and even PTSD in severe cases.

- Victims of identity theft may encounter legal complications, such as being held responsible for fraudulent debts or having their identities used to commit other crimes. Navigating the legal system can be a complex and frustrating process, adding to the stress of recovering from identity theft.

Section 4: Protecting yourself from identity theft

To protect yourself from identity theft, it's essential to be cautious with your personal information. Here are some helpful suggestions:

- Be mindful of what you share online, and properly dispose of sensitive documents using secure data transmission methods.

- Regularly checking your bank and credit card statements for suspicious activity can help you detect signs of identity theft early on. Monitoring your credit reports is also essential, as they can reveal if someone has opened accounts or incurred debts in your name.

- Using strong, unique passwords for your accounts is crucial in protecting your identity. Multi-factor authentication, which requires an additional step to verify your identity (such as a code sent to your phone), can also provide an extra layer of security.

- Being aware of common phishing techniques and scams can help you avoid falling victim to identity theft. Be cautious with unsolicited emails or messages, and never provide personal information to an unverified source.

Smart Tip

Social media is often flooded with fun quizzes and questionnaires that seem harmless but can be used to extract personal information. Be wary of sharing information that could be used as security questions for your accounts, such as your pet's name, your mother's maiden name, or the street you grew up on. Identity thieves can use this information to access your accounts or answer security questions.

Section 5: What to do if you become a victim of identity theft

Immediate steps to take upon discovering identity theft If you suspect you've been a victim of identity theft, act quickly:

- Contact your financial institutions to report the issue, place a fraud alert on your credit reports, and file a report with your local police and the Federal Trade Commission (FTC).
- Notify other relevant organizations, such as the IRS or the Social Security Administration, depending on the nature of the theft. This can help prevent further damage and aid in your recovery process.
- Once you've addressed the immediate concerns, it's time to focus on rebuilding your credit and restoring your identity. This may involve disputing fraudulent charges, closing unauthorized accounts, and diligently monitoring your credit reports to ensure no new fraudulent activity occurs.
- Use your experience as a lesson in the importance of protecting your personal information. Implement the practices you've learned to prevent identity theft and share your knowledge with others to help them avoid similar situations.

Section 6: Educating others about identity theft and prevention

Sharing knowledge and experiences with peers, family, and community Talking openly about your experience with identity theft and sharing the prevention strategies you've learned can help others avoid falling victim to this crime.

- Encourage discussions about online safety in your peer group, family, and community.
- Fostering a cybersecurity awareness and responsibility culture is crucial in preventing identity theft. Encourage those around you to take online safety seriously and to stay informed about the latest threats and prevention methods.
- Open communication and education are vital to raising awareness about identity theft. Support initiatives to educate young people about online safety and encourage dialogue in schools, clubs, and other community settings.

Section 7: Be aware and be safe

Awareness of identity theft risks and prevention methods is an important life skill that may come into play several times throughout your life.

So, understanding the risks associated with identity theft and knowing how to protect yourself is vital to maintaining your security in the digital age. Here are some tips:

- Stay informed about the latest threats and prevention techniques to protect your personal information.

- Proactively safeguarding your personal information can help you avoid becoming a victim of identity theft. Regularly review your accounts, use strong passwords, and be cautious with the information you share online.

- As technology evolves and new threats emerge, staying current on the latest cybersecurity developments is important. Continue learning about online safety and sharing your knowledge with others to create a safer digital environment for everyone.

Smart Tip

Setting up a Google Alert for your name can help you monitor online mentions and quickly detect any suspicious activity related to your personal information. By receiving notifications when your name appears in search results or on websites, you can stay aware of potential risks and take action to protect yourself from identity theft. This can also help you keep track of your online reputation and ensure that your digital footprint remains positive and secure.

Identity theft is a pervasive issue that impacts millions each year. Protecting your personal information and staying informed about identity thieves' latest methods is essential.

By implementing strong security practices, monitoring your financial accounts and credit reports, and sharing your knowledge with others, you can help create a safer digital environment for yourself and your community.

Chapter 17

Future-Proofing Your Cyber Life

Keeping Up with Cybersecurity Trends and Threats

As you become more digitally connected, staying ahead of the curve and protecting yourself from evolving cybersecurity threats is essential. This chapter will cover staying informed about emerging risks, adapting to new technologies and security measures, developing a lifelong learning mindset for cybersecurity, and exploring resources for staying updated on cybersecurity news and trends.

Section 1: Staying Informed About Emerging Cybersecurity Risks

Cyber threats continually evolve, and staying informed about new risks is crucial. Here are some tips for keeping up with emerging cybersecurity risks:

- Follow reputable cybersecurity news sources: Regularly read articles from reliable news outlets and blogs that cover cybersecurity issues.
- Join online cybersecurity communities: Participate in forums, social media groups, and other online communities dedicated to cybersecurity discussions.
- Attend cybersecurity events and conferences: Attend local or online events and conferences to learn from experts and stay informed about the latest trends.
- Engage with your school or local community: Participate in cybersecurity-related clubs or workshops at your school or within your local community.

Smart Tip

Many organizations and educational institutions host cybersecurity competitions, which can be an engaging way to learn about new trends and test your skills. Keep an eye out for such events, and consider forming a team with your peers to participate and learn together.

Section 2: Adapting to New Technologies and Security Measures

As technology advances, new security measures and tools become available. Stay ahead by adapting to these changes:

- Learn about new security features: Regularly research and familiarize yourself with the latest security features for your devices and online accounts.
- Update your devices and software: Ensure you're using the most recent versions of operating systems, apps, and antivirus software, as they often include essential security updates.
- Be open to change: Embrace new security measures and tools as they become available, even if they require changing your habits or routines.
- Educate your friends and family: Share your knowledge with others to help them protect their digital lives as well.

Section 3: Developing a Lifelong Learning Mindset for Cybersecurity

Maintaining a lifelong learning mindset can help you stay on top of the ever-changing cybersecurity landscape. Here's how to foster this mindset:

- Set learning goals: Establish specific cybersecurity education objectives to help guide your efforts and motivate you.

- Embrace curiosity: Promote an interest in understanding how technology works, its risks, and the best practices for staying safe.
- Learn from your mistakes: When you encounter a cybersecurity issue or make a mistake, take it as an opportunity to learn and improve.
- Seek learning opportunities: Regularly participate in workshops, courses, or online tutorials to deepen your cybersecurity knowledge.

Section 4: Resources for Staying Up to Date on Cybersecurity

A variety of resources can help you stay informed about the cybersecurity news and trends:

- News websites: Follow reputable news outlets that cover cybersecurity, such as Wired, Krebs on Security, and Dark Reading.
- Cybersecurity blogs: Subscribe to blogs from cybersecurity experts or companies like the SANS Institute, TrendMicro, marklynd.com, and Norton LifeLock.
- Podcasts: Listen to cybersecurity-themed podcasts like "The CyberWire," "Darknet Diaries," and "Security Now!"
- Social media: Follow cybersecurity influencers, experts, and organizations on social media platforms like Twitter and LinkedIn to stay informed about the latest news and trends.

- Online courses and certifications: Explore cybersecurity courses and certifications from platforms like Coursera, edX, and Cybrary to deepen your knowledge.

Smart Tip

Many experts in the field of cybersecurity maintain an active presence on social media platforms such as Twitter, YouTube, or LinkedIn. Following these influencers will give you regular updates on the latest cybersecurity trends and access to their expert insights and opinions. For instance, you can follow me (the author), as I am one of the top-ranked global cybersecurity thought leaders and influencers and publish a lot of helpful cybersecurity content.

We have covered the importance of staying informed about emerging cybersecurity risks, adapting to new technologies and security measures, developing a lifelong learning mindset, and utilizing various resources to keep current on cybersecurity news and trends. By actively engaging in your cyber education and staying informed about the latest threats and trends, you can confidently navigate the digital world and maintain a secure online presence throughout your teenage years and into adulthood.

Chapter 18

Balancing Act

Understanding and Managing Your Digital Footprint

Section 1: What is a digital footprint and why it matters

Welcome to the age of the internet, where every click, like, and share leave a trace. Your digital footprint is the trail of information you leave behind as you use the internet. It can include anything from your social media posts to your online searches and even the websites you visit. In today's digital world, it's essential to understand how your online actions impact your digital footprint and, ultimately, your reputation.

Your digital footprint matters because it can influence how people perceive you online and offline. Potential employers, colleagues, and even friends may form opinions about you based on your digital footprint. It's essential to manage your online presence carefully to ensure that it reflects the best version of yourself.

Section 2: Strategies for managing your online presence

You'll need to take a proactive approach to manage your online presence effectively. Here are some strategies to help you stay in control of your digital footprint:

- Be mindful of what you share: Before you post something online, ask yourself if it's something you'd be comfortable sharing with a future employer or college admissions officer. If the answer is no, think twice before hitting "post."

- Regularly review your privacy settings: Social media platforms often update their privacy settings, so keeping an eye on them is essential. Regularly review your settings and adjust them to ensure you share information only with the intended audience.

- Search yourself: Conduct regular searches of your name to see what information is publicly available about you. This can help you identify and address potential issues with your digital footprint.

- Limit your public information: Be selective about the information you share online. The more personal details you post, the easier for someone to piece together a comprehensive picture of you.

Smart Tip

As a teen, consider developing a personal brand to present yourself consistently and professionally across all online platforms. This could include having a unique username, creating a logo or avatar, and using the same profile picture across all accounts. A cohesive personal brand can help showcase your interests, talents, and values, ultimately building a positive and reputable digital footprint.

Section 3: The impact of your digital footprint on future opportunities

Your digital footprint can have lasting consequences on your future opportunities. Employers and colleges increasingly use the internet to research candidates, and a negative digital footprint could hurt your chances of being hired or accepted.

For example, imagine you've applied for your dream job or college program. The hiring manager or admissions officer looks you up online and finds inappropriate posts or photos. This could lead them to question your judgment, maturity, or professionalism and ultimately decide not to offer you the position or acceptance.

The key is to be aware of the potential impact of your online actions and make informed decisions about what you share and how you present yourself online.

Section 4: Tips for reducing and controlling your digital footprint

Managing your digital footprint can seem overwhelming, but with a few simple tips, you can take control and make a positive impression online. Here are some ideas to help you reduce and control your digital footprint:

- Delete old accounts: If you have accounts on websites or social media platforms that you no longer use, consider deleting them to reduce the amount of personal information available about you online.

- Clean up your social media profiles: Go through your social media profiles and remove any posts, photos, or comments that don't align with the image you want to present.

- Be cautious with app permissions: When you download a new app, pay close attention to the permissions it requests. Some apps may request access to your personal information or location, even if it's unnecessary for the app's function. Be cautious about granting permissions to protect your privacy.

- Educate yourself about privacy tools: Familiarize yourself with tools like Virtual Private Networks (VPNs), which can help protect your online privacy by encrypting your internet connection and masking your IP address.

By taking control of your digital footprint, you can ensure that your online presence reflects the best version of yourself and supports your future goals. Remember, the internet is an incredible resource, but using it responsibly and thoughtfully is essential.

With a proactive approach to managing your digital footprint, you'll be well-prepared to navigate the online world and positively impact others.

Section 5: Building good digital habits for the future

As you continue to grow and develop, it's crucial to establish good digital habits that will serve you well into adulthood. Here are some suggestions for cultivating positive online behavior:

- Be respectful and empathetic: Remember that real people are behind the screens, and your words and actions can impact others. Treat others with respect and empathy, just as you would want to be treated.

- Think before you post: Consider the potential consequences of your online actions for yourself and others. If you need clarification on whether something is appropriate to post, it's better to err on the side of caution.

- Prioritize online safety: Keep your personal information secure by using strong passwords, enabling two-factor authentication, and being cautious about the websites you visit and the apps you download.

- Balance your online and offline life: While the internet offers many benefits and opportunities, it's essential to maintain a healthy balance between your online and offline life. Take breaks from screens, engage in face-to-face interactions, and participate in hobbies or activities outside of the digital world.

- To create a positive digital footprint, seek online opportunities to contribute to your community or advocate for an important cause. Participate in online forums, join social media groups, or write blog posts highlighting your dedication to a particular issue or charity.

Smart Tip

Schedule periodic reviews of your online presence to ensure your digital footprint remains positive and current. This could involve deleting old or irrelevant posts, untagging yourself from questionable content, or updating your privacy settings. By being proactive and continuously monitoring your online presence, you'll be more likely to maintain a positive and reputable digital footprint throughout your teenage years and beyond.

You should be developing good digital habits now; you'll be better equipped to manage your online presence and make informed decisions about your digital footprint.

By taking control of your online presence, you can ensure that your digital footprint supports your future goals and helps you maintain a positive reputation. Embrace the responsibility of being a digital citizen, and use the strategies and tips outlined in this chapter to build a strong foundation for your online life.

Chapter 19

Trust but Verify

Evaluating Online Sources and Spotting Misinformation

Section 1: The prevalence of misinformation and its consequences

Welcome to the age of information, where you have access to an endless stream of content worldwide. However, only some things you read or see online are accurate and trustworthy. Misinformation, or false information that is spread unintentionally, and disinformation, which is false information spread deliberately to deceive, are all too common on the internet.

The consequences of misinformation can range from misunderstandings and confusion to more severe outcomes, such as influencing public opinion, perpetuating stereotypes, or even causing harm. As a responsible digital citizen, developing the skills to evaluate online sources and spot misinformation is essential.

Section 2: Techniques for evaluating the credibility of online sources

In order to determine whether an online source is credible and reliable, consider the following questions:

- Who is the author or creator? Look for information about the author or organization behind the content. Are they an expert in the field or reputable source? If you can't find any information about the author, that's a red flag.

- What is the purpose of the content? Determine whether the content is meant to inform, persuade, entertain, or sell something. This can help you identify potential biases or agendas.

- When was the content published or updated? Check the publication date and look for signs that the content is up to date. Outdated information can be misleading or inaccurate.

- Where does the information come from? Look for sources, citations, or links to support the claims made in the content. If the information is not supported by evidence, be cautious.

- How does the content make you feel? Be aware of your emotions while consuming content. If the information evokes strong emotions, like fear or anger, it could be intentionally designed to manipulate your feelings and reactions.

Smart Tip

Recognize that your personal beliefs and opinions can influence your perception of information. When you encounter information that confirms your views, please resist the urge to accept it at face value. Instead, take a step back and critically assess whether the information is accurate, regardless of whether it aligns with your beliefs.

Section 3: Fact-checking tools and resources

When in doubt, turn to reliable fact-checking tools and resources to verify the information you encounter online. Some reputable fact-checking websites include:

- Snopes (www.snopes.com): This long-established website investigates urban legends, rumors, and claims to determine their accuracy.
- FactCheck.org (www.factcheck.org): This nonpartisan, nonprofit organization monitors the factual accuracy of political statements and claims made by politicians, political ads, and news articles.
- PolitiFact (www.politifact.com): PolitiFact is another nonpartisan fact-checking organization that rates the accuracy of statements made by politicians and political groups.

- Media Bias/Fact Check
  (www.mediabiasfactcheck.com): This website assesses
  the bias and reliability of various news sources, helping
  you understand the potential biases of the information
  you consume.

Section 4: Developing critical thinking skills for discerning truth from falsehood

Building critical thinking skills is crucial for navigating the vast information available online. Here are some tips for honing your critical thinking abilities:

- Always question what you read: Take only some of
  what you see online at face value. Be curious and ask
  questions about the information you encounter.
- Check multiple sources: Compare information from
  different sources to get a more balanced and accurate
  understanding of a topic or issue.
- Recognize logical fallacies: Learn about common logical
  fallacies, such as ad hominem attacks, straw man
  arguments, and false dilemmas, so you can identify
  them in the content you consume.

Smart Tip

When encountering unfamiliar or suspicious information online, practice lateral reading by opening a new tab and researching the claims from different sources. Don't just rely on the website where you found the information, but actively search for other perspectives, expert opinions, or official sources to verify the credibility of the content.

Learning to evaluate online sources and spot misinformation is vital in today's digital world. By developing critical thinking skills and using reliable fact-checking tools, you can become a more discerning and responsible consumer of information. This will help you make better-informed decisions and contribute to a healthier online environment for everyone.

Chapter 20

Take off with a Career in Cybersecurity

Section 1: Introduction to careers in cybersecurity

In today's digital age, the need for skilled cybersecurity professionals has never been greater. As cyber threats evolve and become more sophisticated, the demand for experts to protect our digital lives grows. For teens, early exposure to the world of cybersecurity can provide a valuable foundation for an exciting and rewarding career.

- The increasing reliance on technology has led to a surge in cybercrime, creating a need for skilled professionals to defend against these threats. As a result, the cybersecurity field has seen significant growth and is expected to continue expanding in the coming years. With millions of job openings worldwide, this presents a unique opportunity for young people to enter a high-demand profession with promising career prospects.

- Getting acquainted with cybersecurity at an early age helps teens develop essential skills and knowledge that will benefit them in their future careers. Exposure to this field also allows teens to explore their interests, build a strong foundation, and gain a competitive edge in the job market.

Section 2: Overview of various cybersecurity career paths

The world of cybersecurity offers a wide array of career paths, each with unique challenges and rewards. Let's examine some of this exciting field's most common career options.

- Ethical hackers, also known as penetration testers, use their skills to test and identify computer systems, networks, and application vulnerabilities. They aim to find security weaknesses before cybercriminals do and help organizations strengthen their defenses.
- Security analysts monitor networks and systems, detect potential threats, and respond to security incidents. They analyze data to identify cyberattack patterns and trends, helping organizations build more robust defenses.
- Cybersecurity engineers design, build, and maintain secure networks, systems, and applications. They develop and implement security policies, standards, and procedures to ensure an organization's digital assets' confidentiality, integrity, and availability.
- Cybersecurity managers and consultants oversee the development and execution of security strategies,

ensuring that organizations are protected against cyber threats. They also provide guidance and expertise to help businesses meet their security objectives and comply with relevant laws and regulations.

- Professionals in this field focus on developing, analyzing, and enforcing laws and regulations related to cybersecurity. They work to shape public policy, protect individual privacy rights, and ensure that organizations comply with legal requirements.

- Educators and researchers in cybersecurity play a crucial role in advancing our understanding of the field. They teach courses, develop training programs, and conduct research to uncover new insights and develop innovative solutions to emerging threats.

Section 3: Education and skill requirements for cybersecurity careers

A successful career in cybersecurity requires a solid educational foundation, technical skills, and personal qualities.

- While it's definitely possible to enter the field with a high school diploma and relevant experience, many cybersecurity professionals hold degrees in computer science, information technology, or a related field. Additionally, industry certifications such as CompTIA Security+, Certified Information Systems Security Professional (CISSP), and Certified Ethical Hacker (CEH) can help demonstrate your expertise and commitment to the field.

- Depending on the specific career path, you may need to be proficient in programming languages, networking, operating systems, or cryptography (encryption, etc.). Familiarity with security tools and software, such as firewalls, intrusion detection systems, and vulnerability scanners, is also essential.

Smart Tip

Take advantage of alternative educational paths. Many cybersecurity professionals come from diverse backgrounds, such as computer science, mathematics, or liberal arts. Consider pursuing certifications, online courses, or workshops to acquire relevant skills and knowledge. This flexibility and openness to learning can make you an attractive candidate to potential employers and help you stand out from the crow should you pursue a career in cybersecurity.

In addition to technical skills, cybersecurity professionals need a range of soft skills and personal qualities to succeed in their careers. These include:

- Critical thinking and problem-solving: Identifying and addressing security threats requires the ability to analyze complex situations and develop effective solutions.
- Attention to detail: Small oversights can have significant consequences in cybersecurity, so

professionals must be thorough and meticulous in their work.

- Communication skills: Cybersecurity experts must be able to clearly explain complex concepts to non-technical colleagues and collaborate effectively with team members.
- Adaptability and flexibility: The fast-paced, ever-changing nature of the cybersecurity landscape requires professionals to be adaptable and open to learning new skills and technologies.

Section 4: The value of hands-on experience and extracurricular activities

Practical experience is essential for building a successful cybersecurity career. Participating in internships, volunteering, or working on personal projects can help you develop your skills and gain valuable hands-on experience. Additionally, extracurricular activities such as joining cybersecurity clubs, attending conferences, and participating in competitions can help you build your network and stay current with industry trends.

Section 5: Tips for exploring and pursuing a cybersecurity career

If you're considering a career in cybersecurity, here are some tips to help you get started:

- Joining clubs or participating in cybersecurity competitions can help you build your skills, network with professionals, and gain exposure to various aspects of the field. Many schools and organizations host hackathons, workshops, and conferences where you can learn from experts and connect with like-minded peers.

- Networking with cybersecurity professionals can provide valuable insights into the field and help you discover potential job opportunities. Attend industry events, join online forums or contact professionals on social media platforms like LinkedIn to start building your network.

- Many online resources are available to help you learn about cybersecurity and develop your skills. Websites like Coursera, edX, and Cybrary offer free and paid courses covering a wide range of cybersecurity topics. Blogs, podcasts, and YouTube channels can also provide valuable information and insights into the field.

- Keeping current with the latest developments in cybersecurity is essential for staying ahead in the field. Regularly read industry news, subscribe to newsletters, and follow cybersecurity experts on social media to stay informed.

Section 6: The future of cybersecurity careers

As technology continues to evolve, so will the cybersecurity landscape. To remain competitive in the job market, professionals must stay informed about emerging trends, such as artificial intelligence, machine learning, and quantum computing.

- Adaptability and a commitment to lifelong learning are crucial for success in the cybersecurity field. Professionals must be prepared to embrace new technologies, learn new skills, and adapt to the ever-changing threat landscape.

- As a cybersecurity professional, you'll play a vital role in safeguarding our digital lives and shaping the future of technology.

- Potential to make a lasting impact not only on the organizations you work for but also on society as a whole. As our reliance on technology continues to grow, so does the importance of ensuring the security and privacy of our digital world.

Cybersecurity is an exciting, challenging, and rewarding career choice for those with the right skills and mindset. With the ever-increasing demand for skilled professionals, the opportunities for growth and advancement in the field are vast. By starting your cybersecurity journey early, you'll be well-positioned to capitalize on these opportunities and contribute to a safer, more secure digital future.

In Closing

As you reach the end of this book, let's take a moment to reflect on the journey we've taken together through the world of cybersecurity. We've explored various topics and skills crucial for navigating the digital landscape safely and responsibly. By acquiring and practicing these skills, you're setting yourself up for success and contributing to a safer and more secure online environment.

Section 1: Recap of the key cybersecurity skills covered in the book

Throughout this guide, we've touched on many critical aspects of cybersecurity, from creating strong passwords to spotting phishing attacks, using social media safely, protecting your devices, and maintaining your privacy online. We've also delved into understanding your digital footprint, evaluating online sources, and staying informed about emerging cybersecurity trends and threats.

Each of these chapters provided you with essential knowledge and practical tips to help you build a strong foundation in cybersecurity. Applying these principles in your daily digital life can reduce risks, protect your information, and help you confidently navigate online.

Four essential skills and habits:

1. Create a strong, unique password for each of your accounts
2. Enable MFA
3. Exercise caution in what you share online.
4. Keep your devices and applications up to date.

Section 2: Encouragement to continue learning and practicing good cybersecurity habits

As with any skill, practice makes perfect. The more you use and reinforce the cybersecurity principles discussed in this book, the more comfortable and proficient you'll become. Staying safe online is an ongoing process that requires regular attention and adaptation.

So, keep exploring, learning, and practicing good cybersecurity habits. Stay curious and always be willing to learn more about the digital world and its potential risks. Doing so will protect you and help you become a role model for your friends and family, inspiring them to follow suit.

Section 3: The lifelong benefits of being cybersecurity-savvy

Being cybersecurity-savvy is a life skill that will serve you well for years. As our world becomes increasingly interconnected, the importance of safeguarding your digital presence will only grow. Your ability to navigate the digital landscape confidently and securely will have far-reaching benefits, from applying for jobs to managing your finances and maintaining healthy relationships.

Moreover, proactively protecting your digital life can help create a more secure online environment for everyone. Your actions, however small they may seem, can have a ripple effect contributing to the global fight against cyber threats.

Section 4: A call to action for teens to be proactive in safeguarding their digital lives

Now, it's time to take what you've learned and put it into action. Embrace your role as a digital citizen and become an advocate for cybersecurity within your community. Please share your knowledge with your friends, family, and peers, and encourage them to take their digital safety seriously as well.

Remember, we all have a part to play in creating a safer online world, and your efforts can make a significant difference. By staying informed, practicing good cybersecurity habits, and encouraging others to do the same, you can help build an exciting and secure digital future.

Thank you

We hope that "Cybersecurity Life Skills for Teens" has provided you with valuable information and practical advice to help you confidently navigate the digital landscape. As you continue your journey toward becoming a more responsible and self-reliant digital citizen, we encourage you to apply the lessons you've learned in this book and share your newfound knowledge with your friends, family, and community.

Thank you, and remember: your cyber safety is in your hands!

Acknowledgments

The author would like to thank the following people and organizations whose dedication and care toward the education and welfare of our teens deeply inspired and motivated me:

The 100's of dedicated and inspirational educators and administrators

All my fantastic colleagues at Netsync

Special thanks to the leadership team at Netsync: Khalid, Len, Jeff, Karl, Kurt, Diana, Beau, Cory, Yong, and Shawn

The amazing team at Houston ISD

Scott Gilhousen

The amazing team at San Antonio ISD

Jaime Aquino, Kenneth Thompson, and Evangelina Mendoza

The amazing team at Lewisville ISD

Bryon Kolbeck

The amazing team at Socorro ISD

Hector Reyna, Alice Ramos

The amazing team at Etiwanda SD

Hillsborough County Public Schools

The amazing team at Lake Travis ISD

Chris Woehl

The amazing team at Jenks Public Schools

The amazing team at Katy ISD

Joe Christoffersen

The amazing Team at MORENet

Matt Parris

The amazing team at McAllen ISD

The amazing team at Shawnee Heights USD

The amazing team at Prosper ISD

Fernando De Velasco

The amazing team at Boerne ISD

The amazing team at Education Service Center Region 20

Patti Holub

The amazing team at Education Service Center Region 11

Tom Call

The amazing team at Education Service Center Region 7

Steve Vaughn

The amazing team at Education Service Center Region 1

Daniel Ramirez

The amazing team at TETL

The amazing team at Leander ISD

David Plummer

Marc Jabian and Netsync Cybersecurity team

Onalytica

Global Thought Leaders: Shira Rubinoff, Chuck Brooks, Jo Peterson, Bob Carver, Spiros Margaris, Dez Blanchfield, Scott Schober, Sally Eaves, Helen Yu, Spiros Margaris, Ronald Van Loon, Theodora Lau, Evan Kirstel, Harold Sinnott, Rob May, and Jim Marous

Thinkers360

And so many more… You are all appreciated!

Many of the Illustrations within this book by GetIllustrations

About Author

Mark Lynd is a well-known expert in tech and cybersecurity with over 24 years of experience. He is the Head of Digital Business and part of the executive team at Netsync, a global technology provider.

He's achieved some pretty cool things in his career, like being a finalist for the "E&Y Entrepreneur of the Year - Southwest Region," presenting the Doak Walker Running Back Award on ESPN's College Football Awards Show and being named the #1 Global Security Thought Leader in 2022 by Thinkers360. Onalytica has also recognized him as one of the top cybersecurity experts and speakers.

In his position at Netsync, Mark helps advise all sorts of public and private organizations on technology and cybersecurity issues. He's incredibly passionate about working with over 250 K12 schools and universities across the United States to ensure they're safe and secure from cyber threats and have a credible incident response capability.

Mark has held significant leadership roles throughout his career, including CEO, CIO, CTO, and CISO for global companies. He's also been a part of several recognized academic and technology boards, including SMU's Cox School of Business.

Mark is an in-demand speaker who often shares his cybersecurity, artificial intelligence, cloud, diversity, STEM, and veteran affairs knowledge for big names like Oracle, IBM Watson, Cisco, HP, SailPoint, AT&T, and Intel.

Mark earned a Bachelor of Science degree from the University of Tulsa and attended the prestigious Wharton School. He's also a proud military veteran, having served with the US Army's 3rd Ranger Battalion & 82nd Airborne. His diverse background and dedication to excellence make Mark the perfect author to help you learn and grow in the world of technology and cybersecurity.